Microwave

Microwave

Bloomsbury Books
London

This edition published 1995 by Bloomsbury Books,
an imprint of The Godfrey Cave Group,
42 Bloomsbury Street, London, WC1B 3QJ.

ISBN 1 85471 587 9

Printed and bound in Great Britain

Contents

Pork and Bean Sprout Soup

Serves 4

Working time: about 30 minutes

Total time: about 1 hour

Calories 245
Protein 30g
Cholesterol 75mg
Total fat 5g
Saturated fat 2g
Sodium 490mg

½ tsp	Sichuan peppercorns, or freshly ground black pepper to taste	½ tsp
500 g	lean pork, julienned	1 lb
¼ tsp	cayenne pepper	¼ tsp
¼ tsp	ground ginger	¼ tsp
2 tbsp	Chinese black vinegar or balsamic vinegar	2 tbsp
1 litre	unsalted brown stock	1¾ pints
1	onion, thinly sliced	1
6	garlic cloves, thinly sliced	6
250 g	bean sprouts	8 oz
1.25 kg	ripe tomatoes, skinned, seeded and chopped, or 800 g (28 oz) canned tomatoes, drained and crushed	2½ lb
4 tbsp	chopped fresh parsley	4 tbsp
2 tbsp	low-sodium soy sauce or shoyu	2 tbsp

Toast the Sichuan peppercorns, if you are using them, in a heavy frying pan over medium-high heat until they smoke—about 2 minutes; using a mortar and pestle, grind them to a powder. Combine the pork with the ground peppercorns or black pepper, cayenne pepper, ginger and vinegar in a small bowl. Let the mixture stand at room temperature for 30 minutes.

Pour the stock into a 2 litre (3½ pint) glass bowl. Add the onion and garlic, and cover the bowl with a lid. Microwave the liquid on high for 10 minutes. Remove the bowl from the oven

and stir the mixture. Cover the bowl again and cook the liquid on high for 10 minutes more.

Meanwhile, place the bean sprouts in a colander and blanch them by pouring about 2 litres (3½ pints) of boiling water over them. Set the bean sprouts aside.

Stir the pork and its marinade into the cooked broth. Microwave the mixture on high until it barely begins to boil, then cook on high for 3 minutes. Add the tomatoes, parsley, soy sauce and blanched bean sprouts. Cook the soup, uncovered, for 3 minutes more on high. Serve immediately.

Broccoli Soup with Cumin and Scallops

Serves 8

Working time: about 20 minutes

Total time: about 50 minutes

Calories 140
Protein 8g
Cholesterol 30mg
Total fat 7g
Saturated fat 4g
Sodium 280mg

30 g	unsalted butter	**1 oz**
500 g	broccoli, florets cut off, stems peeled and cut into 2.5 cm (1 inch) lengths	**1 lb**
2	leeks, split, washed thoroughly to remove all grit, and thinly sliced	**2**
1	large potato, peeled and cut into 1 cm ($\frac{1}{2}$ inch) pieces	**1**
1	garlic clove, finely chopped	**1**
2 tsp	fresh thyme, or $\frac{1}{2}$ tsp dried thyme freshly ground black pepper	**2 tsp**
$\frac{3}{4}$ tsp	salt	**$\frac{3}{4}$ tsp**
1 litre	unsalted chicken stock	**1$\frac{3}{4}$ pints**
$\frac{3}{4}$ tsp	ground cumin	**$\frac{3}{4}$ tsp**
2 tbsp	fresh lemon juice	**2 tbsp**
12.5 cl	single cream	**4 fl oz**
250 g	queen scallops, firm white connective tissue removed	**8 oz**

Put half of the butter into a 4 litre (7 pint) casserole. Add the broccoli, leeks, potato, garlic, thyme and some pepper. Cover the casserole with a lid or plastic film, then microwave on high for 5 minutes.

Add the salt, stock, $\frac{3}{4}$ litre (1$\frac{1}{4}$ pints) of water and the cumin. Cover the dish leaving a corner open for the steam to escape, then microwave the mixture on high for 15 minutes, stirring every 5 minutes. Stir in the lemon juice and cook the mixture on high for 15 minutes more, stirring every 5 minutes. Let the casserole stand for 10 minutes before puréeing the mixture in

batches in a blender or food processor. Return the purée to the casserole; then stir in the cream. Microwave the mixture on high until it is heated through—about 2 minutes.

In a bowl, microwave the remaining butter on high until it melts—about 30 seconds. Add the scallops and cook on high for 30 seconds; stir the scallops, then cook just until they turn opaque—about 30 seconds more.

Ladle the hot purée into heated individual soup plates; garnish each serving with some scallops and serve the soup immediately.

Chilled Beetroot Soup

Serves 6

Working time:
about 25
minutes

Total time:
about 3 hours
and 25 minutes
(includes
chilling)

Calories
60
Protein
2g
Cholesterol
5mg
Total fat
1g
Saturated fat
trace
Sodium
205mg

125 g	tomatoes, quartered	**4 oz**	**2**	bay leaves	**2**
350 g	raw beetroots, peeled and grated	**12 oz**	**90 cl**	unsalted vegetable stock	**1½ pints**
1	carrot, grated	**1**	**175 g**	thick Greek yogurt	**6 oz**
1	onion, grated	**1**	**½ tsp**	salt	**½ tsp**
1	small potato, peeled and grated	**1**		freshly ground black pepper	

Put the tomatoes in a bowl with 3 tablespoons of cold water. Cover the bowl with plastic film, pulled back at one edge, and cook the tomatoes on high for 3 to 4 minutes, until they are pulpy. Sieve the tomato pulp.

Place the beetroot, carrot, onion and potato in a large bowl. Stir in the sieved tomatoes, the bay leaves and half of the stock. Cover the bowl as before, and cook the soup on high for 25 to 30 minutes, until the vegetables are tender; stir the mixture twice during the cooking time. Remove the bay leaves from the soup, then stir in the remaining stock and leave the soup to cool—30 to 45 minutes.

Ladle a little of the cooled soup into a bowl and stir in the yogurt. When the mixture is smooth, add it to the soup and stir to mix it in evenly. Add the salt and some pepper. Chill the soup for 2 hours, before serving.

Mushroom and Parsley Pâté

Serves 6

Working time: about 25 minutes

Total time: about 24 hours (includes chilling)

Calories 85

Protein 4g

Cholesterol 0mg

Total fat 3g

Saturated fat 1g

Sodium 205mg

1 tbsp	polyunsaturated margarine	1 tbsp
2	garlic cloves, crushed	2
1	large onion, finely chopped	1
625 g	flat mushrooms, wiped and roughly chopped	1¼ lb
20 g	flat-leaf parsley, chopped	¾ oz

	freshly ground black pepper	
1 tbsp	mango chutney, chopped	1 tbsp
2 tbsp	white wine vinegar	2 tbsp
¼ tsp	salt	¼ tsp
90 g	fresh wholemeal breadcrumbs	3 oz

Place the margarine in a large bowl and microwave it on high for 30 seconds, or until it has melted. Stir the garlic and onion thoroughly into the margarine, and cook them on high for 2 minutes.

Stir in the mushrooms, and cook the mixture on high for another 5 minutes. Add half the chopped parsley and some black pepper, mix them in, and cook on high for a further 5 minutes. Stir the chopped mango chutney, wine vinegar and salt into the mushroom mixture, making sure that all the ingredients are thoroughly combined. Cook on high for 5 minutes more, or until all the liquid has evaporated. Mix in the breadcrumbs and the remaining chopped parsley.

Spoon the pâté into a round dish measuring about 15 cm (6 inches) in diameter and 7.5 cm (3 inches) in depth. Press the mixture down lightly with the back of the spoon. Leave the pâté to cool and then chill for about 24 hours to allow the flavours to develop fully.

Tomatoes with a Spinach and Tofu Stuffing

Serves 4

Working (and total) time: about 35 minutes

Calories 150
Protein 9g
Cholesterol 5mg
Total fat 8g
Saturated fat 2g
Sodium 280mg

1 tbsp	flaked almonds	**1 tbsp**
350 g	spinach, stalks removed, leaves washed and finely shredded	**12 oz**
2	beef tomatoes (about 500 g/1 lb)	**2**
60 g	smoked tofu	**2 oz**
1 tbsp	grated Parmesan cheese	**1 tbsp**

2 tbsp	fresh wholemeal breadcrumbs	**2 tbsp**
2 tsp	finely shredded fresh basil, or $\frac{1}{2}$ tsp dried basil	**2 tsp**
	freshly ground black pepper	
$\frac{1}{8}$ tsp	salt	**$\frac{1}{8}$ tsp**
1 tbsp	virgin olive oil	**1 tbsp**

In a heavy frying pan, toss the almonds over high heat until they are golden-brown—about 1 minute.

Put the shredded spinach leaves in a bowl, cover them loosely with plastic film or with a lid, and microwave them on high for 3 minutes. Transfer the cooked spinach to a colander to drain thoroughly. Press the leaves gently to remove as much water as possible.

While the spinach drains, halve the tomatoes horizontally, scoop out their seeds with a spoon and discard the seeds. Using a sharp knife, cut out and reserve the tomato pulp. Chop 1 tablespoon of the pulp and set it aside; reserve the rest for another use.

To prepare the stuffing, finely chop the tofu and mix it with the spinach, chopped tomato pulp, Parmesan cheese, breadcrumbs, basil and some freshly ground pepper. Season the hollowed-out tomatoes with the salt and more pepper, then press the mixture into them with a spoon. Sprinkle a little of the olive oil over the top of each tomato.

Place the stuffed tomatoes on a serving dish and microwave them, uncovered, on medium low for 5 minutes. Give each tomato a half turn, then microwave them on low until the tomato shells are tender—3 to 5 minutes more.

Garnish the top of each stuffed tomato with the toasted almond flakes and serve hot.

Scallops Anise

Serves 4

Working time:
about 25
minutes

Total time:
about 1 hour
(includes
marinating)

Calories
115
Protein
3g
Cholesterol
40mg
Total fat
2g
Saturated fat
1g
Sodium
100mg

500 g	shelled scallops, bright white connective tisue removed, rinsed under cold water and patted dry	**1 lb**	**7 g**	unsalted butter, softened	**¼oz**
½	fresh lime	**½**	**1 tsp**	anise flavoured liqeur	**1 tsp**
350 g	tomatoes, skinned and seeded and finely chopped	**12 oz**	**1**	small bunch fresh chervil, large stems removed	**1**
			¼tsp	salt	**¼tsp**
				freshly ground black pepper	

Separate the fleshy part of the scallops from their corals. Pierce each coral once to keep it from bursting during cooking. If you are using large scallops, slice them in half horizontally; if you are using the smaller queen scallops, leave thm whole but pierce each one. Marinate the scallops and corals in the lime juice and rind for 45 minutes. Meanwhile, place the chopped tomato in a fine sieve and let it drain for 30 minutes.

Cream the butter and the liqueur with a wooden spoon; se aside.

Spread the chervil on a 30 cm (12 inch) dish and arrange the drained scallops and corals in a single layer on top. Cover the dish with plastic film, leaving a slight opening.

Microwave on high for 1 minute, giving the dish a quarter turn after 30 seconds. Let the scallops rest in a warm place while you prepare their sauce.

Place the anise-flavoured butter in a bowl and microwave on high until the butter sizzles—20 to 30 seconds. Add the tomato to the butter and microwave again on high until the mixture is just heated through—about 30 seconds.

Season the scallops with half of the salt; sprinkle the tomatoes with the remaining salt and some pepper. Divide the tomato mixture among four plates, piling it to one side. Arrange the scallops and some chervil next to the tomatoes, and serve immediately.

Plaice with Lemon and Parsley

Serves 8

Working (and total) time: about 30 minutes

Calories 65
Protein 11g
Cholesterol 35mg
Total fat 2g
Saturated fat 0g
Sodium 125mg

8	plaice fillets (about 125 g/4 oz each), skinned	8
$\frac{1}{8}$ tsp	salt	$\frac{1}{8}$ tsp
	freshly ground black pepper	
1	small onion, very finely chopped	1

2 tbsp	finely chopped parsley	2 tbsp
3 tbsp	fresh lemon juice	3 tbsp
4 tbsp	white wine	4 tbsp
8	thin lemon slices	8

Lay the fillets flat on a work surface, skinned side up. Season them with the salt and some pepper.

In the base of a shallow serving dish, spread out the onion and parsley, and sprinkle with the lemon juice and white wine. Double over each fillet, with the skinned side in, and arrange the fillets on top of the onion and parsley in two overlapping rows. Tuck the lemon slices between the fillets.

Cover the dish loosely with plastic film, then microwave on high until the fish is opaque—

3 to 4 minutes. Rotate the dish once during the cooking time.

Let the fish stand, still covered with plastic film, for 3 minutes. Then remove the film and serve the plaice straight from the dish, spooning a little of the cooking liquid over each fillet.

Editor's Note: The fish and its cooking liquid may also be served cold, garnished with a salad of radicchio leaves.

Stewed Fennel with Ham

Serves 4

Working time:
about 5
minutes

Total time:
about 20
minutes

Calories
130
Protein
8g
Cholesterol
30mg
Total fat
10g
Saturated fat
4g
Sodium
315mg

125 g	ham, trimmed of fat	**4 oz**
8	fennel bulbs	**8**
1 tbsp	finely chopped fresh thyme, or 1 tsp dried thyme	**1 tbsp**

12.5 cl	white wine	**4 fl oz**
4 tbsp	unsalted vegetable stock	**4 tbsp**
	freshly ground black pepper	
30 g	unsalted butter (optional)	**1 oz**

Cut a thin slice off the root of each fennel bulb and trim off the tops of the stems; reserve the feathery fronds.

Put the fennel bulbs, thyme, white wine, vegetable stock, some freshly ground black pepper and the butter, if you are using it, into a dish. Cover and microwave on high until the fennel is cooked through—about 15 minutes.

Meanwhile, cut the ham into fine dice, and add it to the dish 1 minute before the end of the cooking time. Serve garnished with the feathery tops of the fennel, torn into small pieces.

Editor's Note: Chicory or onions can be substituted for the fennel bulbs with equally good results. Allow two whole vegetables per person and cook for only 10 minutes; garnish with chopped parsley.

Cider Pork

Serves 6

Working time:
about 25
minutes

Total time:
about 4 hours
and 30
minutes

Calories
195
Protein
10g
Cholesterol
70mg
Total fat
10g
Saturated fat
4g
Sodium
80mg

750 g	pork fillet, trimmed of fat and cut into 2.5 cm (1 inch) cubes	**1½ lb**
1	garlic clove crushed	**1**
1 tbsp	walnut oil	**1 tbsp**
15 cl	medium dry cider	**¼ pint**
1	orange, grated rind and juice	**1**

2 tsp	fresh lemon juice	**2 tsp**
1 tbsp	fresh thyme, or 1 tsp dried thyme	**1 tbsp**
½ tsp	grated fresh ginger root	**½ tsp**
½ tsp	freshly ground black pepper	**½ tsp**
4 tsp	arrowroot dissolved in 3 tbsp cider	**4 tsp**

In a large casserole, mix together all the ingredients except the pork and the arrowroot mixture. Stir in the pork, cover and leave to marinate in the refrigerator for 4 to 6 hours. Stir the meat once or twice during this time to make sure the cubes are evenly soaked.

Put the covered casserole in the oven and microwave on medium until the meat is tender—about 10 minutes. Stir once during cooking. Pour the arrowroot and cider mixture into the casserole and microwave on high, stirring once during cooking, until the liquid thickens—about 5 minutes. Serve hot.

Vine Leaves Stuffed with Pork and Rice

Serves 4

Working (and total) time: about 30 minutes

Calories 220
Protein 15g
Cholesterol 45mg
Total fat 12g
Saturated fat 4g
Sodium 250 mg

250 g	trimmed leg or neckend of pork, minced	**8 oz**
12	large fresh vine leaves	**12**
90 g	cooked brown rice	**3 oz**
2 tsp	dried oregano	**2 tsp**
¼ tsp	salt	**¼ tsp**
	freshly ground black pepper	
1 tbsp	fresh lemon juice	**1 tbsp**
2 tbsp	virgin olive oil	**2 tbsp**
30 cl	unsalted chicken stock	**¼ pint**
	lemon slices for garnish	

Put the vine leaves in a bowl and cover generously with water. Microwave on high until boiling—about 5 minutes. Leave the bowl to stand for 10 minutes, then remove the vine leaves and trim away the stalks.

Mix together the minced pork, brown rice, oregano, salt and some freshly ground pepper. Place a spoonful of the pork mixture in the centre of each leaf, wrap one end of the leaf over the filling, then the two sides, and roll up into a neat parcel.

Pack the rolled vine leaves tightly in a single layer in an oval casserole dish, with their seams underneath. Pour over the lemon juice, oil and stock, which should almost cover the parcels. Cover the dish and microwave on medium for 10 minutes.

Serve the stuffed vine leaves hot or cold, garnished with the lemon slices. If serving hot, the cooking liquid may be poured over them.

Editor's Note: If you use vine leaves preserved in brine instead of fresh leaves, rinse them first under running cold water to remove the salt.

Chicken Parmesan

Serves 4

Working time:
about 15
minutes

Total time:
about 40
minutes

Calories
370

Protein
33g

Cholesterol
95mg

Total fat
17g

Saturated fat
5g

Sodium
695mg

8	chicken drumsticks, skinned, rinsed and patted dry	8	1	garlic clove, finely chopped	1
1	small onion, chopped	1	1 tbsp	chopped fresh basil, or 1 tsp dried basil	1 tbsp
1	apple, peeled, cored and finely grated	1	¼ tsp	dried oregano	¼ tsp
1 tbsp	safflower oil	1 tbsp		freshly ground black pepper	
35 cl	puréed tomatoes	12 fl oz	45 g	cornflakes, crushed	1½ oz
2 tbsp	tomato paste	2 tbsp	60 g	Parmesan cheese, freshly grated	2 oz
2 tbsp	Madeira	2 tbsp	12.5 cl	plain low-fat yogurt	4 fl oz

Combine the onion and apple with the oil in a bowl. Cover with a paper towel and microwave on high for 1 minute. Stir in the puréed tomatoes, tomato paste, Madeira, garlic, basil, oregano and some pepper. Cover the bowl with a paper towel again and microwave on medium (50 per cent power) for 9 minutes, stirring the sauce three times during the cooking. Remove the bowl from the oven and let it stand.

While the sauce is cooking, prepare the drumsticks. Sprinkle them with some pepper.

Mix the cornflake crumbs and the Parmesan cheese. Dip the drumsticks into the yogurt, then dredge them in the crumb and cheese mixture, coating them evenly. Arrange the drumsticks on a microwave roasting rack with the meatier parts towards the outside. Microwave on high for 15 minutes, turning the dish once half way through the cooking time. Remove the drumsticks and let them stand for 7 minutes; then arrange them on a serving platter. Reheat the sauce on high for 1 minute and pour some of it over the chicken. Pass the remaining sauce separately.

Teriyaki Chicken

Serves 4

Working time:
about 15
minutes

Total time:
about 2 hours

Calories
170

Protein
20g

Cholesterol
75mg

Total fat
9g

Saturated fat
2g

Sodium
120mg

4	large chicken thighs, skinned and boned	4
2 tbsp	low-sodium soy sauce, or naturally fermented shoyu	2 tbsp
1 tbsp	dry sherry	1 tbsp
$\frac{1}{2}$ tsp	honey	$\frac{1}{2}$ tsp
1	garlic clove, sliced	1
1 tbsp	finely chopped fresh ginger root	1 tbsp
$\frac{1}{8}$ tsp	crushed black peppercorns	$\frac{1}{8}$ tsp
1	spring onions, white part chopped and green part sliced diagonally	1

To prepare the marinade, combine all the ingredients except the chicken and green spring onion slices in a deep bowl. Add the thighs and stir to coat them evenly. Marinate the thighs for 2 hours at room temperature or overnight in the refrigerator.

When you are ready to cook the chicken, preheat a microwave browning dish on high for the maximum time allowed in the instruction manual. Remove the chicken from the marinade, wiping off and discarding the garlic, ginger and spring onion. Set the thighs on the browning dish and microwave them on high for 3 minutes. Turn the pieces over, sprinkle them with the green spring onion slices, and cook them on high for 90 seconds more. Serve immediately.

Editor's Note: If you do not have a microwave browning dish, cook the chicken in an uncovered baking dish for 5 to 6 minutes.

Turkey Ring

Serves 6

Working time:
about 20
minutes

Total time:
about 35
minutes

Calories
265

Protein
23g

Cholesterol
45mg

Total fat
3g

Saturated fat
12g

Sodium
315mg

500 g	turkey breast meat, cut into 5 cm (2 inch) cubes	**1 lb**	**2 tbsp**	chopped fresh basil, or 1 tsp dried marjoram	**2 tbsp**
1	small onion, finely chopped	**1**		freshly ground black pepper	
3 tbsp	virgin olive oil, plus 1 tsp	**3 tbsp**	**1**	green courgette, julienned	**1**
75 g	dry breadcrumbs	**2½ oz**	**1**	yellow squash or courgette, julienned	**1**
17.5 cl	semi-skimmed milk	**6 fl oz**	**1**	sweet red pepper, julienned	**1**
12.5 cl	plain low-fat yogurt	**4 fl oz**	**2**	garlic cloves, finely chopped	**2**
4 tbsp	Parmesan cheese, freshly grated	**4 tbsp**	**¼ tsp**	salt	**¼ tsp**

Combine the onion and 3 tablespoons of the oil in a bowl. Cover with plastic film and microwave on high until the onions are translucent—about 3 minutes.

Mince the turkey in a food processor and mix in the breadcrumbs, milk and yogurt. Add the onion, cheese, 1 tablespoon of the basil or ½ teaspoon of the marjoram, and some pepper. Operate the processor in short bursts to combine the ingredients.

With your hands, press the turkey mixture round the edges of a round dish 25 cm (10 inches) in diameter, forming a ring with a 10 cm (4 inch) diameter hollow at the centre.

Cover tightly with plastic film, leaving a corner open for steam to escape, and microwave on high for 6 minutes, turning the dish a quarter turn every 2 minutes. Let the turkey ring stand while you cook the vegetables.

Combine the courgette, squash and red pepper in a bowl with the remaining oil, the remaining basil or marjoram, the garlic, salt and some pepper. Cover with plastic film and microwave on high for 4 minutes, stirring once half way through the cooking time. Arrange some of the vegetables in a thin band around the outside of the turkey ring and mound the remaining vegetables in the centre. Serve hot.

Poussins with Barley Stuffing

Serves 4

Working time:
about 25
minutes

Total time:
about 1 hour

Calories
385
Protein
29g
Cholesterol
95mg
Total fat
20g
Saturated fat
8g
Sodium
435mg

4x500 g	poussins, rinsed and patted dry	**1 lb**
½ tsp	salt	**½ tsp**
100 g	pearl barley	**3½ oz**
4 tbsp	Parmesan cheese, grated	**4 tbsp**
30 g	unsalted butter	**1 oz**
1	small onion, chopped	**1**
75 g	sweet red pepper, chopped	**2½ oz**
2	garlic cloves, finely chopped	**2**
1 tsp	fresh thyme, or ¼ tsp dried thyme	**1 tsp**
90 g	fresh mushrooms, wiped clean and thinly sliced	**3 oz**
	paprika	

Add ¼ teaspoon of the salt to ¼ litre (8 fl oz) of warm water in a small bowl. Microwave on high for 2 minutes. Add the barley and stir. Cook for 9 minutes on high, stirring once after 5 minutes. Remove the bowl from the oven, cover with plastic film, and leave for 10 minutes. Take off the film, add the cheese, and stir.

Put 15 g (½ oz) of the butter in a bowl and microwave it on high for 30 seconds. Stir in the onion, red pepper, garlic and thyme. Cook for 1 minute on high. Add the mushrooms and the remaining salt, and mix well. Cook on high for 2 minutes, then mix with the barley.

Fill the body cavity of each bird with one quarter of the stuffing, taking care not to pack it tightly. Sew the cavities shut with a needle and heavy thread. Tuck the wing tips under the birds and tie each pair of legs together. Wrap each bird in plastic film and place breast side down in a baking dish. Cook the birds on high for a total of 12 minutes, turning them over every 4 minutes.

Remove the birds from the oven and unwrap them. Melt the remaining butter in a small bowl by microwaving it on high for 30 seconds. Brush each bird with melted butter and sprinkle liberally with paprika. Replace the birds on the dish, breast side up. Microwave them on high for a total of 12 minutes more, turning them every 4 minutes. Let the birds stand for about 5 minutes before serving.

Vegetable Stew with Mange-Tout and Mustard

Serves 6 as a side dish

Working (and total) time: about 25 minutes

Calories
70
Protein
2g
Cholesterol
10mg
Total fat
4g
Saturated fat
2g
Sodium
95mg

1	courgette, halved lengthwise and cut diagonally into 5 mm (¼ inch) slices	**1**
1 tbsp	fresh lemon juice	**1 tbsp**
30 g	unsalted butter, cut into pieces	**1 oz**
2	carrots, cut diagonally into 5 mm (¼ inch) thick ovals	**2**
1	shallot, finely chopped	**1**
1 tbsp	Dijon mustard	**1 tbsp**
1	cos lettuce, cored, the leaves torn into 5 cm (2 inch) pieces	**1**
1 tsp	fresh thyme, or ¼ tsp dried thyme	**1 tsp**
⅛ tsp	salt	**⅛ tsp**
	freshly ground black pepper	
125 g	mange-tout, any stems and strings removed, large pods halved diagonally	**4 oz**

Put the courgette slices into a small bowl, toss the with the lemon juice, and set the bowl aside.

Put the butter into a large bowl and microwave it on high until it melts—about 1 minute. Stir in the carrots, shallot and mustard. Cook the mixture on high for 2 minutes, stirring half way through the cooking time.

Add the lettuce, thyme, salt and some pepper; stir the vegetables to coat them with the butter. Microwave the stew on high for 1 minute, stirring once after 30 seconds. Stir in the courgette slices and lemon juice, then the mange-tout. Cook the stew on high for minutes more, stirring once half way through the cooking time. Stir the vegetables one last time, cover the bowl and let the stew stand for another 3 minute before serving it.

Sweet-and-Sour Fish Stew

Serves 4

Working (and total) time: about 50 minutes

Calories 215
Protein 25g
Cholesterol 40mg
Total fat 1g
Saturated fat 0g
Sodium 175mg

2	carrots, julienned	2
4	spring onions, trimmed and cut into 1 cm (½ inch) lengths	4
1 tbsp	chopped fresh ginger root	1 tbsp
¼ tsp	dark sesame oil	¼ tsp
½ litre	fish stock	16 fl oz
1 tbsp	sugar	1 tbsp
2 tbsp	cornflour, mixed with 3 tbsp water	2 tbsp
2 tbsp	rice vinegar or white wine vinegar	2 tbsp
1 tsp	sweet chili sauce, or ½ tsp crushed hot red pepper flakes mixed with 1 tsp golden syrup and ½ tsp vinegar	1 tsp
1 tsp	low-sodium soy sauce or shoyu	1 tsp
4	dried shiitake or Chinese black mushrooms, soaked in boiling water for 15 minutes, stemmed and cut into strips	4
500 g	cod, bass or monkfish fillet, rinsed and cut into 2.5 cm (1 inch) cubes	1 lb
125 g	mange-tout	4 oz
75 g	drained and rinsed bamboo shoots	2½ oz
30 g	cellophane noodles, soaked in hot water for 10 minutes, drained, cut into 5 cm (2 inch) lengths	1 oz

Combine the carrots, spring onions, ginger and oil in a 2 litre (3½ pint) glass bowl. Cover and microwave on medium (50 per cent power) for 3 minutes. Stir in the stock, sugar, cornflour mixture, vinegar, chili sauce or pepper flake mixture, soy sauce and mushrooms. Cover, and cook on high for 3 minutes.

Arrange the fish cubes in a single layer in a shallow baking dish. Distribute the mange-tout, bamboo shoots and noodles on top of the fish. Pour the sweet- and-sour sauce over all, cover, and microwave on high for 2 minutes. Rearrange the fish, moving less-cooked cubes from the centre of the dish to the edges. Cover once more and cook on high until the fish can be easily flaked with a fork—about 2 minutes.

Chicken Ratatouille

Serves 4

Working (and total) time: about 45 minutes

Calories 240
Protein 29g
Cholesterol 70mg
Total fat 5g
Saturated fat 1g
Sodium 345mg

4 tbsp	Madeira	4 tbsp
2 tsp	chopped fresh oregano	2 tsp
1 tsp	chopped fresh rosemary, or	1 tsp
1 tsp	chopped fresh thyme, or	1 tsp
2 tbsp	finely chopped shallot	2 tbsp
2	garlic cloves, finely chopped	2
1 tsp	safflower oil	1 tsp
400 g	canned tomatoes, puréed with their juice in a blender	14 oz
1	small bay leaf	1

350 g	aubergine, cut into chunks	12 oz
2	small courgettes (preferably 1 green and 1 yellow), cubed	2
1	sweet red pepper, seeded, deribbed and cubed	1
1	sweet green pepper, seeded, deribbed and cut squares	1
$\frac{1}{2}$ tsp	salt	$\frac{1}{2}$ tsp
	freshly ground black pepper	
500 g	chicken breast meat, cubed	1 lb

Place the Madeira, oregano, rosemary and thyme in a cup and microwave them on high for 2 minutes. Leave to stand for 5 minutes.

Put the shallot and garlic into a 2 litre (3½ pint) glass bowl; stir in the oil and microwave the mixture on medium (50 per cent power) for 2 minutes. Add the tomato purée, bay leaf, aubergine, courgettes, red pepper, green pepper and the herb mixture. Stir gently to distribute the vegetables, then cover the bowl.

Microwave on high for 8 minutes, stirring once during the process.

Sprinkle the salt and some pepper over the chicken cubes, then stir them into the ratatouille. Cover the bowl and microwave it on high for 5 minutes, stirring once during the process. If the chicken is not white throughout, cook the ratatouille for 1 or 2 minutes more. Remove the bay leaf and transfer the ratatouille to a warmed serving dish. Serve immediately.

Sage-Marinated Lamb Chops

Serves 4

Working time:
about 25
minutes

Total time:
about 1 hour
and 30
minutes

Calories
235
Protein
25g
Cholesterol
75mg
Total fat
12g
Saturated fat
6g
Sodium
175mg

8	loin chops (about 125 g/4 oz each), trimmed of fat	**8**
2 tsp	chopped fresh sage, or ¾ tsp dried sage. crumbled	**2 tsp**
3	garlic cloves, finely chopped	**3**
1 tbsp	brandy	**1 tbsp**
1	lemon, grated rind only	**1**

2 tbsp	balsamic·vinegar, or 1½ tbsp red wine vinegar mixed with ½ tsp honey	**2 tbsp**
1 tbsp	dark brown sugar	**1 tbsp**
¼ tsp	salt	**¼ tsp**
	freshly ground black pepper	

Mix the sage, garlic, lemon rind, vinegar, brown sugar, brandy, salt and some pepper in a 20 cm (8 inch) square glass dish. Add the lamb chops to the dish and turn to coat them with the marinade. Let the lamb chops stand for 1 hour at room temperature, turning them every 15 minutes.

Microwave the chops, uncovered, on high for 2 minutes. Turn the chops over, rearranging them so that the chops that were at the outside of the dish are now at the centre. Cook the chops on high for 3 minutes more. Remove the dish from the oven and cover it loosely with foil. Let the lamb chops stand for 5 minutes before serving them.

Editor's Note: Do not marinate the lamb cubes for more than six hours, otherwise they will become too soft.

Lamb Roast with Winter Vegetables

Serves 8

Working time:
about 30 minutes

Total time:
about 1 hour

Calories
220

Protein
26g

Cholesterol
75mg

Total fat
8g

Saturated fat
3g

Sodium
175mg

2 kg	leg of lamb, fillet end, trimmed and boned	**4 lb**
2 tsp	chili powder	**2 tsp**
1 tbsp	chopped fresh rosemary or 2 tsp dried rosemary, crumbled freshly ground black pepper	**1 tbsp**
600 g	cauliflower, florets	**1¼ lb**
3	carrots, sliced pieces	**3**
500 g	Brussels sprouts, trimmed	**1 lb**
15 cl	unsalted brown or chicken stock	**¼ pint**
¼ tsp	salt	**¼ tsp**
1 tbsp	cornflour, mixed with 2 tbsp water	**1 tbsp**

Rub the chili powder over the joint, then sprinkle it with the rosemary and plenty of pepper. Place the lamb in a roasting bag and tie the bag loosely, leaving an opening for steam. Make sure that the opening faces upwards. Place the lamb in a shallow dish.

Microwave the lamb on medium high for 16 minutes. Turn it over, keeping the juices in the bag; cook for 16 minutes more.

Remove the lamb from the oven and take it out of the roasting bag. Let the roast stand for 10 minutes. Pour the juices from the bag into a large bowl. Set aside. (At this point an instant reading meat thermometer inserted into the centre of the roast should register 77°C/170°F;

if it does not, cook the lamb for another 5 minutes on medium.)

Meanwhile, pour into a large saucepan 2.5 cm (1 inch) water. Put a vegetable steamer in the pan and bring to the boil. Put the vegetables into the steamer, cover and steam the vegetables until tender—about 10 minutes.

Skim the fat off the top of the meat juices. Stir in the stock, salt and cornflour mixture and microwave the sauce on high until it has thickened—about 2 minutes. Stir again.

Slice the meat. Arrange it on a platter surrounded by the vegetables and pour the sauce over all.

Lamb Baked in Saffron Yogurt

Serves 4

Working time: about 30 minutes

Total time: about 4 hours and 45 minutes

Calories 195
Protein 25g
Cholesterol 80mg
Total fat 8g
Saturated fat 3g
Sodium 90mg

600 g	lean lamb (from the leg or loin), trimmed of fat and cut into 2.5 cm (1 inch) cubes	**1¼ lb**
3	garlic cloves, finely chopped	**3**
2 tbsp	finely chopped fresh ginger root	**2 tbsp**
¼ tsp	saffron threads or turmeric	**¼ tsp**
1 tbsp	cornflour	**1 tbsp**
1	fresh hot green chili pepper, seeded, deribbed and finely chopped	**1**
17.5 cl	plain low-fat yogurt	**6 fl oz**
2	spring onions, trimmed and thinly sliced, for garnish	**2**

Put the lamb cubes, garlic, ginger, saffron or turmeric, cornflour, chili pepper and yogurt in a baking dish. Mix the ingredients well together, then cover the dish and refrigerate it for about 4 hours.

Microwave the lamb and its marinade, covered with greaseproof paper, on medium for 15 minutes, stirring the mixture every 5 minutes. Let the dish stand for 5 minutes; stir it once again before serving. Garnish the lamb with the radishes and spring onions.

Editor's Note: Do not marinate the lamb cubes for more than six hours, otherwise they will become too soft.

Butterfly Chops with a Barbecue Sauce

Serves 6

Working (and total) time: about 45 minutes

Calories 270
Protein 28g
Cholesterol 80mg
Total fat 12g
Saturated fat 5g
Sodium 280mg

6	double loin butterfly chops (about 175 g/6 oz each), boned and trimmed of fat, secured with wooden cocktail sticks	**6**
	unpeeled pineapple wedges, for garnish	
	Barbecue sauce	
250 g	fresh pineapple flesh, or unsweetened canned pineapple chunks, drained	**8 oz**

200 g	canned tomatoes, drained and sieved	**7 oz**
3 tbsp	low-sodium soy sauce or shoyu	**3 tbsp**
3 tbsp	clear honey	**3 tbsp**
2 tbsp	red wine vinegar	**2 tbsp**
2	garlic cloves, crushed	**2**
¼ tsp	cayenne pepper	**¼ tsp**
2 tsp	paprika	**2 tsp**
	freshly ground black pepper	

To make the sauce, purée the pineapple flesh in a blender or food processor, then press the purée through a nylon sieve into a large, clean bowl, to remove any stringy pieces. Add the remaining sauce ingredients to the pineapple purée and stir them in well. Cook the sauce, uncovered, on high for 10 minutes, stirring every 2 minutes. Set the sauce aside. Heat a browning dish for the maximum time allowed in the instruction manual. Brown the chops on both sides in the dish, then cover and microwave on high for 3 minutes; turn and rearrange the chops after 1½ minutes. Skim off any fat.

Pour the barbecue sauce over and round the meat. Microwave, uncovered, for 4 minutes, turning and rearranging the chops after 2 minutes. Serve the chops garnished with the pineapple wedges.

Cottage Pie

Serves 6

Working
(and total)
time: about
1 hour and
30 minutes

Calories
250
Protein
22g
Cholesterol
55mg
Total fat
8g
Saturated fat
3g
Sodium
240mg

500 g	lean lamb from fillet end of leg, trimmed of fat and minced	**1 lb**
500 g	potatoes, peeled and sliced	**1 lb**
250 g	carrots, peeled and sliced	**8 oz**
250 g	swede, peeled and sliced	**8 oz**
1 tbsp	safflower oil	**1 tbsp**
1	large onion, halved and thinly sliced	**1**
20 g	plain flour	**¾ oz**
15 cl	unsalted veal stock	**¾ pint**
	freshly ground black pepper	
½ tsp	salt	**½ tsp**
2 tbsp	chopped parsley	**2 tbsp**

Put the potatoes, carrots, and swede into a large microwave-safe mixing bowl with 6 tablespoons of cold water. Cover the bowl with plastic film, leaving a corner open. Microwave on high, stirring every 5 minutes, until the vegetables are softened—about 20 minutes in total. Remove the bowl from the oven and allow the vegetables to stand for 5 minutes.

Meanwhile, heat a browning dish on high for the maximum time allowed in the manufacturer's instructions. Add the oil and the onion. Cover and microwave on high for 2 to 3 minutes, until the onion is softened. Add the minced lamb and cook, uncovered, on high for 2 minutes, stirring every 30 seconds with a fork to break up the meat. Stir in the flour and add the stock. Microwave on high for 3 minutes, stirring every minute. Season with black pepper and half of the salt; stir in the parsley. Spoon the meat into a microwave safe serving dish.

Using a vegetable masher, mash the potatoes, carrots and swede together with any liquid left in the bowl, to produce a creamy purée. Season with some black pepper and the remaining salt. Spoon the vegetable purée evenly over the meat and mark swirls on the surface of the purée with a small palette knife.

Microwave the cottage pie on high for 15 minutes, giving the dish a quarter turn every 5 minutes. Serve the pie immediately.

East African Fish Stew

Serves 4

Working time: about 20 minutes

Total time: about 35 minutes

Calories 435
Protein 22g
Cholesterol 20mg
Total fat 8g
Saturated fat 1g
Sodium 185mg

250 g	fresh tuna (or swordfish)	**8 oz**
1 tbsp	safflower oil	**1 tbsp**
1	large onion, chopped	**1**
2	garlic cloves, finely chopped	**2**
1 tsp	ground turmeric	**1 tsp**
400 g	canned whole tomatoes, coarsely chopped, juice reserved	**14 oz**
1 tsp	red wine vinegar	**1 tsp**
1 tsp	brown sugar	**1 tsp**
20	saffron threads	**20**
⅛ tsp	crushed red pepper flakes	**⅛ tsp**
140 g	long-grain rice	**4½ oz**
¼ tsp	salt	**¼ tsp**
2	waxy potatoes (about 350 g/12 oz) peeled and cut into cubes	**2**
75 g	shelled peas	**2½ oz**
2 tbsp	fresh lemon juice	**2 tbsp**
2 tbsp	garam masala	**2 tbsp**

In a large glass bowl, stir together the oil, onion, garlic and turmeric. Cover the bowl and microwave it on high until the onions are limp—2 to 3 minutes. Stir in the tomatoes and their juice, the vinegar, brown sugar, saffron threads and red pepper flakes. Cover the bowl and microwave it on high for 10 minutes.

Bring ½ litre (16 fl oz) of water to the boil in a small saucepan; add the rice and salt. Cover the pan and cook over medium heat until all the water has been absorbed—about 20 minutes.

While the rice is cooking, finish the stew.

Rinse the fish under cold running water, pat it dry with paper towels and cut it into 1 cm (½ inch) cubes. Add the potatoes to the onion-tomato mixture. Cover and microwave on high for 5 minutes. Next add the tuna; cover the bowl and microwave it on high for 10 minutes more, stirring half way through. Finally, add the peas and lemon juice and cook the stew on high, covered, for 1 minute.

To serve, divide the rice evenly between four bowls. Ladle one quarter of the stew over each serving of rice. Serve the garam masala separately.

Swordfish Steaks with Lemon, Orange and Lime

Serves 4

Working time: about 15 minutes

Total time: about 35 minutes

Calories 250

Protein 30g

Cholesterol 75mg

Total fat 12g

Saturated fat 3g

Sodium 155mg

750 g	swordfish steak (or shark or tuna) trimmed and cut into quarters	**1½ lb**		½ tsp dried rosemary	
1	lemon	**1**	**1**	bayleaf, crushed	**1**
1	orange	**1**	**½ tsp**	fresh thyme, or ¼ tsp dried thyme	**½ tsp**
1	lime	**1**	**¼ tsp**	fennel seeds	**¼ tsp**
1½ tbsp	virgin olive oil	**1½ tbsp**	**⅛ tsp**	cayenne pepper	**⅛ tsp**
1 tsp	fresh rosemary, crushed, or	**1 tsp**			

Rinse the swordfish steaks under cold running water and pat them dry with paper towels. Cut the lemon, orange and lime in half. Cut one half of each fruit into wedges and reserve the wedges for garnish. Squeeze the juice from the other halves into a small bowl. Pour the citrus juices over the fish and let the fish marinate at room temperature for 30 minutes.

While the fish is marinating, pour the oil into a 12.5 cl (4 fl oz) ramekin. Add the rosemary, bay leaf, thyme, fennel seeds and cayenne pepper. Cover the ramekin with plastic film and microwave it on high for 2 minutes. Set the seasoned oil aside until the fish finishes marinating.

Preheat the microwave browning dish on high for the maximum time allowed in the manufacturer's instruction manual. While the dish is heating, brush the seasoned oil on both sides of each swordfish steak. When the dish is ready, set the steaks on it and cook them on high for 90 seconds. Turn the steaks over and cook them for 90 seconds more—they will still be translucent in the centre. Let the steaks stand for 1 minute, then serve them with the fruit wedges.

Editor's Note: If you do not have a microwave browning dish, microwave the steaks in an uncovered baking dish for 5 to 6 minutes.

Oysters and Pasta Shells in Mornay Sauce

Serves 4

Working (and total) time: about 20 minutes

Calories **335**
Protein **21g**
Cholesterol **90mg**
Total fat **12g**
Saturated fat **4g**
Sodium **315mg**

250 g	shucked oysters, drained	**8 oz**
125 g	medium pasta shells	**4 oz**
1 tbsp	safflower oil	**1 tbsp**
1 tbsp	finely chopped shallot	**1 tbsp**
60 g	Gruyère cheese, coarsely grated	**2 oz**
2 tbsp	flour	**2 tbsp**

¼ litre	semi-skimmed milk	**8 fl oz**
	grated nutmeg	
⅛ tsp	salt	**⅛ tsp**
	white pepper	
1 tbsp	fresh breadcrumbs	**1 tbsp**
½ tsp	paprika	**½ tsp**

Cook the pasta in 1 litre (1¾ pints) of boiling water with ¼ teaspoon of salt; start testing the shells after 10 minutes and cook them until they are *al dente*. Drain, put them in a bowl and cover them with cold water.

Place the oil and shallot in another bowl, cover with plastic film or a lid, and microwave it on high for 45 seconds. Toss the cheese with the flour, evenly coating the cheese, and add this mixture to the bowl. Stir in the milk, a pinch of nutmeg, the salt and some white pepper. Cover the bowl again, leaving a slight gap to allow steam to escape, and microwave it on high for 3 minutes. Remove from the oven and stir the sauce.

Drain the reserved pasta and combine it with the sauce. Gently stir in the oysters, then transfer the mixture to a shallow baking dish. Cover the dish and microwave it on medium (50 per cent power) for 5 minutes. Remove the dish from the oven and stir to blend the oyster liquid into the sauce. Combine the breadcrumbs with the paprika and sprinkle them over the top. Serve immediately.

Prawn Teriyaki

Serves 4

Working time:
about 20
minutes

Total time:
about 30
minutes

Calories
125
Protein
17g
Cholesterol
130mg
Total fat
1g
Saturated fat
0g
Sodium
405mg

500 g	large raw prawns, peeled and deveined	**1 lb**	**1 tsp**	cornflour	**1 tsp**
4 tbsp	sweet sherry	**4 tbsp**	**12.5 cl**	fish stock or dry white wine	**4 fl oz**
2 tbsp	low-sodium soy sauce or shoyu	**2 tbsp**	**1**	carrot, peeled and julienned	**1**
1 tsp	rice vinegar	**1 tsp**	**3**	spring onions, trimmed and cut into 5 cm (2 inch) pieces, the pieces thinly sliced lengthwise	**3**
1	garlic clove, finely chopped	**1**			
1	slice wholemeal bread	**1**			

Combine the sherry, soy sauce, vinegar and garlic in a bowl. Add the prawns and stir gently to coat them evenly. Marinate the prawns in the refrigerator for 20 minutes, stirring them from time to time.

Microwave the slice of bread on high for 2 minutes. Place the bread in a polythene bag and crush it into crumbs with a rolling pin.

Mix the cornflour with 1 tablespoon of the stock or wine. Strain the marinade into a glass bowl; stir in all but 2 tablespoons of the remaining stock or wine, along with the cornflour mixture. Microwave this sauce on high for 3 minutes. Stir the sauce until it is smooth, then set it aside.

Dip the prawns into the breadcrumbs to coat them on one side. Arrange the prawns, coated side up, in a shallow dish. Pour in the remaining stock or wine. Cover the dish and microwave it on high for 3 minutes. Rearrange the prawns, turning any uncooked pieces towards the edge of the dish.

Stir the carrot and spring onion strips into the sauce; pour the sauce around the prawns. Cover the dish again and cook it on medium high (70 per cent power) for 2 minutes. Allow the prawns to stand, covered, for another 2 minutes before transferring them to a serving dish. Spoon the sauce and vegetables around the prawns and serve immediately.

Crab Meat with Tomatoes, Mushrooms and Garlic

Serves 4

Working (and total) time: about 25 minutes

Calories
215
Protein
22g
Cholesterol
85mg
Total fat
5g
Saturated fat
1g
Sodium
245mg

500 g	crab meat, picked over	**1 lb**
250 g	mushrooms, cleaned and sliced	**½ lb**
6	shallots, finely chopped	**6**
6	garlic cloves, finely chopped	**6**
6 tbsp	dry sherry	**6 tbsp**
6 tbsp	dry white wine	**6 tbsp**

⅛ tsp	crushed red pepper flakes	**⅛ tsp**
500 g	ripe tomatoes, skinned, seeded and chopped	**1 lb**
2 tbsp	chopped fresh parsley	**2 tbsp**
1 tbsp	virgin olive oil	**1 tbsp**

Combine the mushrooms, shallots, garlic, sherry, wine and crushed red pepper flakes in a baking dish. Cover and microwave on high for 8 minutes, stirring once mid-way through the cooking time. Add the crab meat, tomatoes, parsley and oil, and toss well. Cover the dish tightly, microwave on high for 2 minutes and serve immediately. (If you prefer, spoon individual portions into ceramic or natural crab shells before serving.)

Mussels in Peppery Red-Wine Sauce

Serves 4
as a first
course

Working
(and total)
time: about
15 minutes

Calories
165

Protein
14g

Cholesterol
75mg

Total fat
6g

Saturated fat
1g

Sodium
315mg

1 kg	mussels, scrubbed and debearded	**2 lb**
2	large shallots, finely chopped	**2**
2	garlic cloves, finely chopped	**2**
1	bayleaf	**1**
⅛ tsp	dried thyme	**⅛ tsp**

25	black peppercorns (about ½ tsp), crushed with the flat of a knife	**25**
12.5 cl	red wine	**4 fl oz**
1 tbsp	red wine vinegar	**1 tbsp**
1 tbsp	olive oil	**1 tbsp**

Place half of the mussels, the shallots, garlic, bay leaf, thyme, peppercorns and wine in a deep dish. Cover and microwave it on high for 2 minutes. Set aside the mussels that have opened. If there are any that remain closed, re-cover the dish and microwave it on high for 30 seconds more. Again set aside the open mussels. Microwave any remaining unopened mussels on high for 30 seconds. Discard any that stay closed. Add the remaining mussels to the dish and cook them in the same way.

When all of the mussels have been cooked, pour the vinegar and oil into the dish, cover it, and microwave the mixture on high for 2 minutes. Return the mussels to the dish, stirring to coat them with the liquid, and cover the dish once more. Microwave on high for 1 minute to heat the mussels through. Serve the mussels in their shells directly from the dish, or transfer them to a serving bowl along with their sauce.

Spinach and Salmon Canapés

Makes 12
canapés

Working time:
about 25
minutes

Total time:
about 30
minutes

Per canapé:
Calories
90
Protein
9g
Cholesterol
25mg
Total fat
4g
Saturated fat
1g
Sodium
140mg

250 g	salmon steak, skinned and boned	8 oz	1	small sweet red pepper, pricked all over with a fork	1
2	egg whites	2			
175 g	skinned sole or plaice fillets	6 oz	175 g	spinach leaves, stemmed, washed and drained	6 oz
2 tbsp	quark	2 tbsp			
6	slices wholemeal bread	6			

Finely chop the salmon in a food processor, then blend in one egg white. Tip the mixture into a bowl. Repeat this procedure with the sole or plaice and the second egg white. Stir 1 tablespoon of the quark into each of the mixtures and chill them.

Place the red pepper on a paper towel in the microwave oven and microwave on high for 4 minutes, turning after every minute. Put the pepper in a small bowl, cover with plastic film and leave to cool. Peel off the skin and remove the seeds, then cut out 12 small diamond shapes from the flesh. Set aside.

Put the spinach leaves in a bowl, cover and microwave on high for 4 minutes. Drain well, taking care not to break up the leaves.

Line the hollows of two plastic egg cartons with plastic film. Divide the sole mixture equally among the 12 moulds and smooth the surface. Divide the spinach leaves into 12 portions and arrange each portion in an even layer over the sole. Top the spinach with an even layer of the salmon mixture. Cook one box at a time on high for 1½ to 2 minutes, until the fish mixtures are just firm to the touch.

Meanwhile, toast the bread and cut out 12 circles with a 4.5 cm (1¾ inch) round cutter.

Put a plate over each carton and invert it to remove the fish moulds; drain off any liquid. Lift each mould on to a circle of toast and place a red pepper diamond on top. Serve the assembled canapés warm.

Vegetable Purées in Chicory

Makes about
50 leaves

Working time
about 40
minutes

Total time:
about 1 hour

Per leaf:
Calories
60
Protein
2g
Cholesterol
0mg
Total fat
2g
Saturated fat
trace
Sodium
90mg

300 g	carrots, peeled and sliced	**10 oz**
1	orange, grated rind of half, juice of whole	**1**
350 g	Brussels sprouts, trimmed	**12 oz**
350 g	potatoes, scrubbed well, dried and picked all over with a fork	**12 oz**
175 g	fromage frais	**6 oz**

1 tsp	ground coriander	**1 tsp**
¼ tsp	white pepper	**¼ tsp**
¾ tsp	salt	**¾ tsp**
1 tbsp	hazelnut oil	**1 tbsp**
¼ tsp	grated nutmeg	**¼ tsp**
1	bunch flat-leaf parsley, chopped	**1**
4	heads chicory	**4**

Place the carrots, orange rind and juice in a dish. Cover with plastic film, leaving one corner open, and microwave on high until the carrots are tender—about 8 minutes. Cool.

Place the sprouts with 4 tablespoons of water in another dish. Cover with plastic film, leaving one corner open, and microwave on high until just soft—6 to 8 minutes. Cool.

Space the potatoes out on paper towels in the oven. Microwave on high for 10 minutes, turning half way through cooking. Leave for 2 minutes; if they are not soft, microwave 2 to 5 minutes more. Cool, then remove the skins.

In a food processor, chop the carrots. Add 45 g (1½oz) of the *fromage frais*, the coriander,

white pepper and ¼ teaspoon of the salt, and purée.

Remove the carrot purée from the processor and clean the bowl. Process the sprouts until finely chopped, then add the oil, nutmeg and ¼ teaspoon of the salt, and purée. Add 30 g (1 oz) of the *fromage frais* and blend to form a very smooth purée. Mash the potatoes, then beat them with the parsley and the remaining *fromage frais* and salt.

Separate the chicory leaves, and wash and dry them carefully. Using a piping bag fitted with a large star nozzle, fill one third of the leaves with each of the vegetable purées. Serve.

Diced Lamb with Pink Grapefruit and Tarragon

Serves 4

Working time: about 30 minutes

Total time: about 45 minutes

Calories 340

Protein 35g

Cholesterol 75mg

Total fat 11g

Saturated fat 6g

Sodium 310mg

500 g	lean lamb (from the leg or loin), trimmed and cut into cubes	**1 lb**
1½	pink grapefruits	**1½**
125 g	spring onions, trimmed and cut diagonally into 2.5 cm (1 inch) pieces	**4 oz**
3 tbsp	dry white vermouth	**3 tbsp**
1 tbsp	chopped fresh tarragon, or 1 tsp dried tarragon	**1 tbsp**
750 g	spinach, washed, stems removed	**1½ lb**
2 tbsp	cornflour	**2 tbsp**
1 tsp	clear honey	**1 tsp**
¼ tsp	salt	**¼ tsp**
	freshly ground black pepper	
4 tbsp	crème fraîche	**4 tbsp**

Squeeze out and reserve the juice from the half grapefruit. Remove and discard the skin and white pith from the remaining grapefruit, then carefully cut out the flesh from between the membranes and set the segments aside.

Put the lamb, grapefruit juice, spring onions, vermouth and tarragon in a 2.25 litre (4 pint) casserole dish and stir. Cover with a lid, or with plastic film pulled back at one corner, and microwave on medium for 15 minutes, stirring every 5 minutes. Remove the casserole from the oven and leave it to stand.

Shake off any excess water from the spinach and put it in a large bowl. Cover with plastic film, pulling back one corner, and cook on high until wilted and tender—5 to 6 minutes. Drain well, squeezing out as much water as possible, and chop it roughly. Arrange round the edge of a microwave-safe serving dish.

Blend the cornflour with 2 tablespoons of water and stir into the lamb, with half of the grapefruit segments and the honey. Cook, uncovered, on high for 5 minutes, stirring twice, then stir well once more. Season the lamb, add the remaining grapefruit segments and stir in the *creme fraîche*. Spoon into the centre of the spinach and reheat on high for 2 minutes. Serve.

Stuffed Chops with Kidney Bean - Juniper Sauce

Serves 4

Working time:
about 20
minutes

Total time:
about 35
minutes

Calories
425

Protein
40g

Cholesterol
70mg

Total fat
15g

Saturated fat
5g

Sodium
110mg

4	pork chops (about 150 g/5 oz each), trimmed of fat	4
30 g	pine-nuts	1 oz
60 g	cooked long-grain rice	2 oz
4	fresh dates, stoned	4
½ tsp	dried rosemary	½ tsp
1 tsp	safflower oil	1 tsp

	Kidney bean and juniper sauce	
250 g	cooked kidney beans	8 oz
¼ tsp	freshly ground black pepper	¼ tsp
18	juniper berries	18
30 cl	unsalted vegetable stock	½ pint
2 tbsp	tomato paste	2 tbsp

In a food processor, blend together the pine-nuts, rice, dates and rosemary. Cut a cavity in the side of each of the chops, and press the stuffing mixture into the cavities.

Preheat a browning dish for 5 to 7 minutes, or for the maximum time allowed in the manufacturer's instructions, and swirl the oil round the base of the dish. Pat the chops dry with paper towels to facilitate browning, and arrange them in the dish with the thickest part to the outside, pressing them down on to the browning surface with a spatula. When the sizzling stops, cook the chops on high for 1 minute before turning them over to brown the other side.

To make the sauce, purée the kidney beans, pepper, juniper berries, stock and tomato paste in a food processor or blender. Pour into a shallow dish and arrange the chops over the purée with the thicker part towards the outside of the dish.

Microwave on high, uncovered, until the chops are just cooked—about 7 minutes. Remove the chops from the dish and keep them warm.

Return the dish to the microwave and cook the sauce on high for 3 minutes to reduce and thicken it, stirring once during cooking. Pour the sauce on to the chops and serve immediately.

Celery Chops

Serves 4

Working time: about 15 minutes

Total time: about 40 minutes

Calories
200

Protein
25g

Cholesterol
70mg

Total fat
9g

Saturated fat
4g

Sodium
390mg

4	boneless loin chops (about 125 g/4 oz each), trimmed	**4**
350 g	celery, cut into pieces	**12 oz**
15 cl	stout	**¼ pint**
15 cl	unsalted vegetable stock	**¼ pint**
½	onion, sliced	**½**
1 tsp	arrowroot, dissolved in 1 tbsp stout, stock or water	**1 tsp**

90 g	smetana	**3 oz**
1 to 2 tbsp	prepared English grainy mustard	**1 to 2 tbsp**
1 tbsp	torn lovage leaves	**1 tbsp**
1 tbsp	torn celery leaves	**1 tbsp**
½ tsp	salt	**½ tsp**
	freshly ground black pepper	

Place the celery in a dish with the stout, stock and onion. Bring to the boil on high, then cook on high for 10 to 15 minutes, or until tender.

Preheat a browning dish on high for 5 to 7 minutes, or for the maximum time allowed in the manufacturer's instructions. Place the chops in the dish with the thickest part to the outside and press down with a spatula. Once the sizzling stops, cook on high for 1 minute, then turn to brown the other side lightly.

Pour the celery and cooking liquid round the chops and cook on high or until the liquid bubbles. Reduce to medium and cook for 3 minutes, covered, giving the dish a quarter turn

every minute. Allow to rest for 2 minutes, then test by cutting through the thickest part of a chop with a sharp knife; if the meat is still pink, cook for 1 minute more and test as before. When fully cooked, drain the pork and celery, reserving the cooking liquid, and keep warm.

Beat the arrowroot mixture into the smetana, then stir in 1 tablespoon each of the mustard and reserved cooking liquid. Cook on high for 1 to 2 minutes, until thickened, stirring. Add the lovage and celery, salt, pepper, and the remaining mustard to taste. Pour over the pork and celery and serve.

Winter Fruited Chops

<table>
<tr><td>Serves 4</td></tr>
<tr><td>Working (and total) time: about 30 minutes</td></tr>
</table>

<table>
<tr><td>Calories
180</td></tr>
<tr><td>Protein
25g</td></tr>
<tr><td>Cholesterol
70mg</td></tr>
<tr><td>Total fat
8g</td></tr>
<tr><td>Saturated fat
3g</td></tr>
<tr><td>Sodium
260mg</td></tr>
</table>

4	loin chops (about 125 g to 150 g/4½ to 5 oz) trimmed of fat	4
2 tbsp	English grainy mustard	2 tbsp
12	fresh sage leaves	12
½ tsp	salt	½ tsp
2	slices Seville orange, halved	2
2 tsp	fine mustard powder (optional)	2 tsp
4 tbsp	cranberry sauce or preserve	4 tbsp
200 g	fresh cranberries, chopped	7 oz
2 tbsp	port	2 tbsp
	freshly ground black pepper	

Cut a pocket in the boneless side of each chop. Spread ½ tablespoon of the mustard over the surfaces of each pocket, and press three sage leaves on to the mustard. Sprinkle with a little and place a half slice of orange in each pocket.

Dust one side of each chop with ½ teaspoon of the mustard powder, if you are using it. Spread 1 tablespoon of the cranberry sauce over the powdered side of each chop and press the fresh berries firmly into the preserve.

Arrange the chops in a dish with the thickest part to the outside. Microwave on medium for 4 minutes, turning once, then rearrange the chops ensure a even cook. Cook for a further 6 to 8 minutes on medium, giving the dish a quarter turn at least three times.

Remove the chops from the oven, rest them in their dish for 2 minutes, then test to see if done by cutting into the bone end of a chop with the point of a sharp knife; if no pink meat is visible, the chops are cooked through. If the meat still appears pink, cook for a further 1 to 2 minutes on medium, then test as before. Remove the chops from the dish and keep them warm.

To make a quick, light sauce, reduce the cooking juices in the dish by microwaving on high for 2 to 3 minutes; add the port wine and reduce further until slightly syrupy in appearance. Season with the remaining salt and some black pepper, and spoon over the chops.

Fettuccine alla Carbonara

Serves 4

Working (and total) time: about 20 minutes

Calories
440
Protein
19g
Cholesterol
90mg
Total fat
18g
Saturated fat
8g
Sodium
470mg

250 g	fettuccine	**8 oz**
100 g	lean rindless back bacon rashers	**3½oz**
15 cl	semi-skimmed milk	**¼ pint**
10 cl	low-fat single cream	**3½ fl oz**
15 g	Parmesan cheese, freshly grated	**½oz**

1	egg and 1 egg white	**1**
	freshly ground black pepper	
15 g	unsalted butter	**½oz**
2	garlic cloves, crushed	**2**
	finely chopped parsley, to garnish	

Cover a large heatproof plate with a double thickness of absorbent kitchen paper. Arrange the bacon rashers in a single layer on the paper, then cover them with a double thickness of absorbent paper. Microwave on high for 2 to 2½ minutes until the bacon is cooked. Chop the bacon into small pieces and set aside.

Pour 2½ litres (4 pints) of boiling water into a large bowl, add 1½ teaspoons of salt and the fettuccine. Microwave on high for 10 to 12 minutes until the pasta is *al dente*, stirring every 3 minutes. Drain, cover and keep warm.

In a small bowl, lightly whisk together the cream, milk, Parmesan cheese, egg and egg white. Season with pepper, and set aside.

Put the butter into a large bowl and microwave on high for 30 seconds, until melted. Add the garlic and bacon, and microwave for a further 1 minute.

Add the egg and cream mixture to the garlic and bacon. Microwave for 2 to 2½ minutes, stirring every 30 seconds until the mixture is very hot, and slightly thickened. Add the pasta and mix well. Pour into a large warm serving bowl, sprinkle with parsley and serve immediately.

Pasta Shells with Clams and Sweetcorn

250 g	medium pasta shells	**8 oz**
16	medium-sized clams, scrubbed	**16**
22 g	unsalted butter	**¾ oz**
2	spring onions, sliced thinly	**2**
90 g	sweetcorn kernels	**3 oz**

3 tbsp	plain flour	**3 tbsp**
¼ pint	semi-skimmed milk	**15 cl**
1 tbsp	paprika, preferably Hungarian	**1 tbsp**
⅛ tsp	cayenne pepper	**⅛ tsp**
2 tbsp	freshly grated Parmesan cheese	**2 tbsp**

Put 4 tablespoons of water into a 2 litre (3½ pint) bowl. Cover the bowl with a lid and microwave on high for 1 minute. Add the clams, cover again and microwave on high until the clams have partially opened—about 2 minutes. Discard any that remain closed. Drain and leave the clams to cool.

Pour 1.25 litres (2 pints) of hot water into another 2 litre (3½ pint) bowl. Cover and microwave on high until the water boils. Add ½ teaspoon of salt and the pasta shells to the water. Cover, leaving a small opening for steam, and microwave on high for 2 minutes. Stir the pasta and again creating a vent. Return the bowl to the oven. Microwave on medium until the shells are *al dente*—about 5 minutes more. Drain thoroughly and set it aside.

Microwave the butter in a large bowl and on high for 1 minute. Add the spring onions and sweetcorn, cover and cook on high for 1 minute.

Shell the clams over their bowl to catch any juices. Allow the sediment to settle to the bottom of the bowl. Reserve 12.5 cl (4 fl oz) of the clam liquid.

Whisk the flour into the onion-sweetcorn mixture stir. Gradually in the milk and reserved clam liquid. Add the paprika and cayenne pepper. Cover and microwave on high for 90 seconds. Uncover, stir and re-cover. and microwave on high for 90 seconds more.

Put the pasta shells and clams in a serving bowl. Pour on the sauce and toss well. Cover the bowl and microwave on high for 1 minute, then sprinkle the cheese over the pasta and serve.

Egg Noodles with Beef and Mushrooms

Serves 4

Working (and total) time: about 20 minutes

Calories
435
Protein
26g
Cholesterol
100mg
Total fat
14g
Saturated fat
7g
Sodium
445mg

250 g	wide egg noodles	**8 oz**
2 tsp	safflower oil	**2 tsp**
15 g	unsalted butter	**½ oz**
250 g	mushrooms, wiped clean, stems trimmed, thinly sliced	**8 oz**
1	small onion, thinly sliced	**1**
250 g	beef fillet, cut into thin strips	**8 oz**
1	garlic clove, finely chopped	**1**

1 tsp	dry mustard, mixed with 1 tsp water	**1 tsp**
1½ tbsp	paprika, preferably Hungarian	**1½ tbsp**
½ tsp	salt	**½ tsp**
	freshly ground black pepper	
4 tbsp	soured cream	**4 tbsp**
12.5 cl	plain low-fat yogurt	**4 fl oz**
4 tbsp	coarsely chopped chives	**4 tbsp**

Cook the noodles in the conventional manner: put them into 3 litres (5 pints) of boiling water on the stove top with 1½ teaspoons of salt. Start testing them after 7 minutes and cook them until they are *al dente*. Drain the noodles, toss them with the oil, and set them aside.

While the noodles are cooking, put the butter in a 2 litre (3½ pint) bowl and cover the bowl with a lid or plastic film. Microwave the butter on high for 30 seconds. Add the mushrooms and onion, and gently toss them until they are coated with the butter. Cover the bowl again and microwave the contents on medium high (70 per cent power) for 2

minutes. Add the beef strips, garlic, mustard, 1 tablespoon of the paprika, the ½ teaspoon of salt and a generous grinding of black pepper to the mushroom-onion mixture. Cover again and microwave on medium high (70 per cent power) for 5 minutes, stirring the mixture half way through the cooking time. Remove the bowl and drain off the liquid that has accumulated in the bottom.

Add the noodles, soured cream and yogurt to the bowl; stir well, cover and microwave it on high for 2 minutes, stirring after 1 minute. Serve hot with the remaining paprika and the chives sprinkled over the top.

Green Fettuccine with Plaice

Serves 4

Working (and total) time: about 25 minutes

Calories
330
Protein
19g
Cholesterol
30mg
Total fat
6g
Saturated fat
1g
Sodium
325mg

250 g	green fettucine	**8 oz**
4 tsp	virgin olive oil	**4 tsp**
2	garlic cloves, peeled and finely chopped	**2**
1 tbsp	chopped fresh oregano	**1 tbsp**
400 g	canned whole tomatoes, drained and coarsely chopped	**14 oz**

12.5 cl	clam juice or fish stock	**4 fl oz**
250 g	plaice or sole fillet, cut into bite-size pieces	**8 oz**
¼ tsp	salt	**¼ tsp**
	freshly ground black pepper	
2 tbsp	freshly grated Parmesan cheese	**2 tbsp**

Pour 1.25 litres (2 pints) of hot water into a 2 litre (3½ pint) glass bowl. Cover the bowl with a lid or plastic film left slightly open to allow the steam to escape, and microwave on high until the water comes to the boil—about 6 minutes. Stir in ½ teaspoon of salt and add the fettuccine; cover the bowl again and microwave it on high, stirring once after 3 minutes, until the pasta is *al dente*—about 6 minutes in all. Drain the fettuccine, then toss it with 2 teaspoons of the oil and set it aside.

In a shallow 1 litre (2 pint) dish, combine the remaining 2 tablespoons of oil with the garlic, oregano and tomatoes. Cover the bowl

with a lid or plastic film and microwave the mixture on medium high (70 per cent power) until it is heated through—about 90 seconds. Uncover the dish and stir in the clam juice or fish stock and the plaice; cover the dish again, leaving a corner open, and microwave it on high until the fish is cooked through and can be easily flaked with a fork—2 to 3 minutes.

Pour the fish mixture over the fettuccine, season with the ¼ teaspoon of salt and some pepper, and toss well. Cover the dish and microwave it on high until it is heated through—about 1 minute. Sprinkle the cheese over the top and serve immediately.

Spaghetti with Garlic, Oregano and Parsley

Serves 4

Working
(and total)
time: about
30 minutes

Calories
290
Protein
8g
Cholesterol
0mg
Total fat
8g
Saturated fat
1g
Sodium
240mg

2	whole garlic bulbs, the cloves separated and peeled	**2**
¼ tsp	chopped fresh oregano, or ⅛ tsp dried oregano	**¼ tsp**
2 tbsp	chopped fresh parsley, preferably flat-leaf	**2 tbsp**
¼ tsp	salt	**¼ tsp**
⅛ tsp	cayenne pepper	**⅛ tsp**
2 tbsp	virgin olive oil	**2 tbsp**
1	lemon, cut into 8 wedges	**1**
250 g	spaghetti	**8 oz**

In a baking dish, combine the garlic, oregano, parsley, salt, cayenne pepper and 12.5 cl (4 fl oz) of water. Cover with a lid or plastic film, leaving one corner open, and microwave the mixture on high for 6 minutes, turning the dish every 2 minutes. Remove the dish from the oven and let it stand for 2 minutes. Purée the mixture and set it aside.

Cook the spaghetti in the conventional manner: add it to 3 litres (5 pints) of boiling water with 1½ teaspoons of salt. Start testing after 10 minutes and cook until *al dente*. Drain and return to the pan. Pour in the oil and toss well. Add the garlic sauce and toss again. Transfer to a serving dish; garnish with the lemon wedges.

Cauliflower Cheese Mould

Serves 6

Working (and total) time: about 50 minutes

Calories 185
Protein 11g
Cholesterol 100mg
Total fat 11g
Saturated fat 6g
Sodium 270mg

1 kg	cauliflower florets	**2 lb**	**½ tsp**	salt	**½ tsp**
45 g	unsalted butter	**1½ oz**		freshly ground black pepper	
45 g	plain flour	**1½ oz**	**¼ tsp**	grated nutmeg	**¼ tsp**
30 cl	skimmed milk	**½ pint**		strips of peeled sweet red	
60 g	Parmesan cheese, grated	**2 oz**		pepper, for garnish	
2	eggs, beaten	**2**		watercress sprigs, for garnish	

Put the cauliflower florets into a very large bowl, add 6 tablespoons of cold water, then cover the bowl with plastic film, pulling it back at one corner. Cook on high for 15 to 20 minutes, stirring every 5 minutes, until the cauliflower is cooked but still slightly firm. Meanwhile, grease a 20 cm (8 inch) round dish. Line the bottom with greased non-stick parchment paper.

Drain any excess water from the cauliflower florets, then process them briefly in a food processor until they are finely broken up but not puréed. Set aside.

Put the butter into a large bowl and microwave it on high for 30 seconds, until melted. Mix in the flour, then gradually stir in the milk. Cook on high for 4 minutes, stirring every minute with a wire whisk, until thick. Remove from the microwave and beat in the Parmesan, eggs, salt, pepper, nutmeg and cauliflower.

Carefully spoon the cauliflower mixture into the prepared dish and level the surface. Cover the dish with plastic film, leaving a corner open. Cook on high for 12 to 15 minutes, until set, giving the dish a quarter turn every 3 minutes.

Remove the cauliflower mould from the oven and allow it to stand for 5 minutes, then carefully turn it out on to a flat serving dish. Garnish with the sweet pepper strips and watercress sprigs. Serve cut into wedges.

Courgette and Tomato Clafoutis

Serves 4	Calories 120
Working (and total) time: about 45 minutes	Protein 9g
	Cholesterol 110mg
	Total fat 4g
	Saturated fat 1g
	Sodium 270mg

2	eggs	**2**
30 g	wholemeal flour	**1 oz**
30 g	plain flour	**1 oz**
2 tbsp	wheat germ	**2 tbsp**
30 cl	skimmed milk	**½ pint**
200 g	cherry tomatoes, pierced with a fine skewer	**7 oz**
250 g	courgettes, sliced into 1 cm (½ inch) rounds	**8 oz**
2	fresh thyme sprigs, leaves only, chopped if large	**2**
8	large basil leaves, torn in strips	**8**
½ tsp	bottled peppercorns, drained and rinsed	**½ tsp**
	freshly ground green pepper (optional)	

In a bowl mix the eggs with the flours and 1 tablespoon of the wheat germ. Whisk in the milk and salt. Rest the batter for 30 minutes.

Brush the base and sides of a 25 cm (10 inch) diameter shallow microwave dish with a little olive oil and sprinkle evenly with the remaining wheat germ. Arrange the tomatoes and courgettes in the dish.

Stir the batter well, then mix in the herbs and peppercorns. Pour the mixture over the vegetables. Cover the dish with plastic film, leaving one corner open. Microwave on medium, stirring the contents of the dish from time to time, until the edges of the batter begin to set—3 to 5 minutes. Then microwave for a further 10 minutes, giving the dish a quarter turn every 3 minutes. Remove the plastic film, place a layer of absorbent paper towel lightly over the surface of the clafoutis and cover it with a fresh piece of plastic film. Allow the clafoutis to stand, covered, for 3 minutes.

The clafoutis should now be set in the centre. If it is not, microwave it on medium for a further 2 to 3 minutes, then allow it to rest for 2 more minutes.

Serve the clafoutis warm, cut into wedges. Grind a little green pepper over each portion if you like.

Mixed Vegetable Pipérade

Serves 4

Working
(and total)
time: about
20 minutes

Calories
120
Protein
5g
Cholesterol
110mg
Total fat
7g
Saturated fat
1g
Sodium
250mg

1 tbsp	virgin olive oil	**1 tbsp**	
¼ tsp	cayenne pepper	**¼ tsp**	
125 g	potatoes, cut into 1 cm (½ inch) cubes	**4 oz**	
125 g	broccoli; cut into small florets, stems peeled and finely sliced	**4 oz**	
1	sweet yellow pepper, seeded, deribbed and cut into squares	**1**	

1	sweet red pepper, seeded, deribbed and cut into squares	**1**	
½ tsp	cornflour, mixed with 1 tsp cold water	**½ tsp**	
½ tsp	salt	**½ tsp**	
2	eggs, beaten	**2**	
1	garlic clove, halved	**1**	
	crushed hot red pepper flakes		

Place the oil and garlic in a wide, shallow dish. Microwave on medium for about 1 ½ minutes, or until the oil is hot and infused with garlic. Discard the garlic and sprinkle the cayenne pepper over the oil. Add the potato cubes, stir them to coat them in oil and spice, then cook them on high, covered with plastic film pulled back at one corner, for 1 minute.

Stir the potato cubes again, then add the broccoli and yellow and red peppers. Cover as before and microwave on high for 5 minutes. Stir the contents of the dish twice during this time, replacing the plastic film each time. After cooking, stir once more and allow the vegetables to rest, covered, for 2 minutes.

Stir the cornflour mixture and the salt into the beaten eggs, then pour this over the vegetables. Stir, and microwave on medium for 3 minutes. Keep the dish covered during cooking but stir every minute. The egg mixture and the juices should be almost set at the end of this time.

Remove the dish from the oven and rest the contents, covered, for a further minute. Serve the pipérade immediately, sprinkled with the crushed red pepper flakes.

Spiced Bean Medley

Serves 6

**Working time:
about 20
minutes**

**Total time:
about 2 hours
and 40 minutes
(includes
soaking)**

**Calories
220**

**Protein
12g**

**Cholesterol
0mg**

**Total fat
4g**

**Saturated fat
0g**

**Sodium
25mg**

125 g	dried red kidney beans, picked over	**4 oz**	**1**	small fresh red chili pepper, seeded and finely chopped	**1**
90 g	dried pinto beans, picked over	**3 oz**	**1**	small fresh green chili pepper, seeded and finely chopped	**1**
60 g	dried black kidney beans, picked over	**2 oz**	**1**	sweet red pepper, seeded, deribbed and cut into strips	**1**
30 g	dried aduki beans, picked over	**1 oz**	**500 g**	tomatoes, skinned, seeded and chopped	**1 lb**
1 tbsp	safflower oil	**1 tbsp**			
2	garlic cloves, sliced	**2**			

Put all the beans into a large casserole, pour in about 2 litres (3½ pints) of boiling water and microwave, uncovered, on high for 15 minutes. Stir the beans, then soak for 1 hour.

Put the oil, garlic, onion, chili peppers and sweet red pepper into a casserole and cook, uncovered, on high, for 3 minutes. Stir in the salt and the tomatoes, then set the sauce aside until needed.

After the beans have soaked, drain them and rinse them well in cold water. Return them to the casserole and cover them with fresh boiling water. Cook the beans, uncovered, on high for

30 minutes, then cook them on medium for a further 50 minutes. At the end of cooking, drain the beans and return them to the casserole, together with the sauce. Cook on high for 3 to 5 minutes, until thoroughly heated through. Stir the medley before serving it.

Editor's Note. To skin tomatoes in the microwave, pierce the skin once or twice, then microwave on high for about 45 seconds, until the skin starts to peel away. The spiced bean medley may also be served cold, in which case a crisp green salad makes a good accompaniment.

Oriental Parchment Parcels

Serves 4

Working (and total) time: about 20 minutes

Calories 110

Protein 5g

Cholesterol 0mg

Total fat 8mg

Saturated fat 0g

Sodium 10mg

4 tsp	sesame oil	**4 tsp**
200 g	firm tofu, cut into 2 cm (¾ inch) cubes	**7 oz**
100 g	fresh shiitake mushrooms, finely sliced	**3½ oz**
75 g	baby sweetcorn, cut into 2.5 cm (1 inch) lengths	**2½ oz**
75 g	courgettes, sliced	**2½ oz**
60 g	young carrots, cut into thin ribbons with a vegetable peeler	**2 oz**
4 tsp	low-sodium soy sauce or shoyu	**4 tsp**
2	large garlic cloves, halved or four small garlic cloves	**2**
5 cm	piece fresh ginger root, cut in half	

Take four sheets of greaseproof or non-stick parchment paper, each about 25 cm (10 inches) square, and brush the centres with 1 teaspoon of the oil.

Divide the tofu cubes and vegetables equally among the four pieces of paper, piling the ingredients on to the oiled section. In a small bowl mix the remaining oil with the soy sauce. Using a garlic press, crush the garlic and ginger and add the pulp and juices to the bowl, discarding any coarse fibres that may have been pushed through the press. Sprinkle a quarter of this mixture over each pile of vegetables.

Bring two facing edges of one of the paper sheets together above the vegetables, and make a double fold in the edges, to seal and join them. Then make a double fold in each of the two open ends, to seal the parcel. Prepare the other three parcels in the same way, and place all four in a wide shallow dish, arranging them towards the outside edges of the dish so that they will cook evenly.

Microwave on high for 4 to 5 minutes, until the vegetables are tender, giving the dish a quarter turn after each minute. Serve as soon as possible, keeping the parcels closed until the moment of serving.

Sweet-and-Sour Tumbled Vegetables

Serves 4

Working time: about 30 minutes

Total time: about 45 minutes

Calories 150
Protein 5g
Cholesterol 0mg
Total fat 5g
Saturated fat 0g
Sodium 25mg

1 tbsp	safflower oil	**1 tbsp**
2	garlic cloves, crushed	**2**
1 tbsp	finely chopped fresh ginger root	**1 tbsp**
250 g	courgettes, ends trimmed, sliced into 5 mm (¼ inch) thick slices	**8 oz**
125 g	okra, stalk ends trimmed	**4 oz**
1	bunch spring onions, roots trimmed, all but 5 cm (2 inches) of green top cut off, sliced into lengths	**1**
1	sweet red pepper, seeded, deribbed and cut into strips	**1**
350 g	fresh pineapple, diced	**12 oz**
1	sweet green pepper, seeded, deribbed and cut into strips	**1**
1	sweet yellow pepper, seeded, deribbed and cut into strips	**1**
1	sweet orange pepper, seeded, deribbed and cut into strips	**1**
125 g	bean sprouts, picked over	**4 oz**
125 g	baby sweetcorn	**4 oz**
1 tsp	clear honey	**1 tsp**
2 tbsp	low-sodium soy sauce or shoyu	**2 tbsp**
15 cl	unsweetened pineapple juice	**¼ pint**

Put the oil, garlic and ginger into a large casserole and microwave on high for 2 minutes. Add all the vegetables, stirring well. Stir the honey, soy sauce and pineapple juice together in a jug or bowl. Pour this sauce over the vegetables and stir in the pineapple.

Cover the casserole with plastic film, leaving one corner open. Microwave on high for 10 to 12 minutes, until the vegetables are cooked but still crisp; during this time, give the casserole a quarter turn every 3 minutes, and stir the contents after 5 minutes' cooking.

Remove the casserole from the oven and allow the vegetables to stand, covered, for 5 minutes. Then stir them once more and serve.

Editor's Note: For best results, select tender young vegetables for this dish. If older vegetables are used, increase the cooking time by 1 to 2 minutes.

Mushroom Quiche

Serves 4

Working time (and total) time: about 40 minutes

Calories 265

Protein 10g

Cholesterol 30mg

Total fat 14g

Saturated fat 6g

Sodium 120mg

125 g	wholemeal flour	4 oz
30 g	unsalted peanut butter	1 oz
30 g	unsalted butter, chilled	1 oz
	Mushroom filling	
175 g	fresh shiitake mushrooms	6 oz
175 g	oyster mushrooms	6 oz

15 g	unsalted butter	½ oz
15 g	wholemeal flour	½ oz
15 cl	skimmed milk	¼ pint
1 tbsp	chopped parsley	1 tbsp
¼ tsp	salt	¼ tsp
	freshly ground black pepper	

To make pastry, put the flour into a mixing bowl and lightly rub in the peanut butter and butter, until the mixture resembles fine breadcrumbs. Using a round bladed knife to mix, add enough cold water to the flour mixture to form a fairly firm dough—about 3 to 4 tablespoons. Turn the dough out on to a work surface dusted with a little flour, and roll it out to line an 18 cm (7 inch) fluted flan dish. This kind of dough is quite crumbly, so use any trimmings to fill in the cracks. Chill the pastry case in the refrigerator for 5 minutes, then line it with a paper towel. Press the towel gently into the contours of the case. Microwave on high for 4 to 5 minutes, until the pastry looks dry.

For the filling, put the mushrooms into a bowl with 2 tablespoons of cold water. Cover with plastic film, leaving one corner open, and cook on high for 2 minutes. Remove from the oven and set aside. In a separate bowl, heat the butter on high for 15 to 20 seconds, or until melted. Stir in the flour and then whisk in the milk. Add the parsley and cook on high for 3 minutes, stirring every minute with a wire whisk. Season with the salt and some pepper, then add the mushrooms and cook on high, covered as before, for a further 3 minutes, stirring after the first minute.

Remove the paper towel from the pastry case, pour in the mushroom filling, and serve immediately.

Picadillo

Serves 6

Working time:
about 45
minutes

Total time:
about 3 hours
(includes
soaking)

Calories
225
Protein
18g
Cholesterol
35mg
Total fat
6g
Saturated fat
1g
Sodium
235mg

500 g	topside of beef, trimmed of fat and minced	**1 lb**
200 g	dried chick-peas, picked over	**7 oz**
1	onion, chopped	**1**
4	garlic cloves, finely chopped	**4**
1 tsp	safflower oil	**1 tsp**
800 g	canned whole tomatoes, drained and crushed	**1¾ lb**

75 g	sultanas	**2½ oz**
12	green olives, stoned and rinsed	**12**
½ tsp	ground cinnamon	**½ tsp**
½ tsp	ground allspice	**½ tsp**
¼ tsp	cayenne pepper	**¼ tsp**
2	bay leaves	**2**

Rinse the chick-peas under cold running water, then put them into a large, heavy saucepan with enough water to cover them by about 7.5 cm (3 inches). Cover the pan, leaving the lid ajar, and slowly bring the liquid to the boil over medium-low heat. Boil the chick-peas for 2 minutes, then turn off the heat, and soak the chick-peas, covered, for at least 1 hour. Return the chick-peas to the boil, reduce the heat, and simmer them until they are tender—about 1 hour.

Combine the chopped onion, garlic and safflower oil in a large bowl, cover the bowl with plastic film and microwave the vegetables on high for 4 minutes. Add the minced beef and cook the mixture, uncovered, on medium (50 per cent power) for 5 minutes. Stir the beef, breaking it into small pieces, and cook it on medium for 3 minutes more.

Drain the chick-peas and add them to the beef mixture. Stir in the tomatoes, sultanas, olives, cinnamon, allspice, cayenne pepper and bay leaves. Cook the picadillo, uncovered, on high for 15 minutes, stirring it every 5 minutes. Remove the bay leaves and let the picadillo stand for 5 minutes before serving.

Meatballs in Caper Sauce

Serves 4 as an appetizer

Working time: about 20 minutes

Total time: about 30 minutes

Calories 120
Protein 14g
Cholesterol 35mg
Total fat 4g
Saturated fat 1g
Sodium 190mg

300 g	topside of beef, trimmed of fat and minced	**10 oz**
1	small onion, chopped	**1**
¼ litre	unsalted brown or chicken stock	**8 fl oz**
4 tbsp	rolled oats	**4 tbsp**
1 tbsp	chopped parsley	**1 tbsp**
¼ tsp	grated nutmeg	**¼ tsp**

1	lemon, grated rind only	**1**
	freshly ground black pepper	
1 tsp	cornflour, mixed with 1 tbsp water	**1 tsp**
1 tbsp	plain low-fat yogurt	**1 tbsp**
1 tsp	soured cream	**1 tsp**
1 tsp	capers, rinsed and chopped	**1 tsp**

Put the onion in a 1 litre (1¾ pint) baking dish. Cover and microwave on high for 3 minutes. Transfer the onion to a bowl. Pour the stock into the baking dish and cook it on high until it comes to a simmer—about 4 minutes.

While the stock is heating, add the beef, rolled oats, ½ tablespoon of the parsley, the nutmeg, the lemon rind and a liberal grinding of pepper to the onion. Knead the mixture then form it into 16 meatballs. Drop the meatballs into the heated stock and cook them, covered, on high for 4 minutes.

Using a slotted spoon, transfer the meatballs to a serving dish. Discard all but 12.5 cl (4 fl oz) of the cooking liquid in the baking dish; stir the cornflour mixture into this remaining liquid. Cook the liquid on high until it thickens—about 30 seconds. Turn off the heat and let the thickened stock cool for 1 minute, then stir in the yogurt, soured cream, capers and the remaining parsley. Pour the sauce over the meatballs and serve them while they are still hot.

Lime-Ginger Beef

Serves 4

Working time:
about 25
minutes

Total time:
about 45
minutes

Calories
240
Protein
25g
Cholesterol
65mg
Total fat
10g
Saturated fat
3g
Sodium
180mg

600 g	rump steak, trimmed of fat and cut into thin strips	**1¼ lb**
	freshly ground black pepper	
1 tbsp	safflower oil	**1 tbsp**
2	spring onions, trimmed and sliced into thin strips	**2**
1	large carrot, julienned	**1**
1	sweet red pepper, seeded, deribbed and julienned	**1**

Lime-ginger sauce

1	lime, grated rind and juice	**1**
1 tsp	grated fresh ginger root	**1 tsp**
2 tbsp	dry sherry	**2 tbsp**
2 tsp	low-sodium soy sauce or shoyu	**2 tsp**
½ tsp	finely chopped garlic	**½ tsp**
1 tbsp	sugar	**1 tbsp**
1 tbsp	cornflour, mixed with 4 tbsp water	**1 tbsp**

Preheat a microwave browning dish on high for the maximum time allowed in the dish's instruction manual. While the dish is heating, combine all the ingredients for the lime-ginger sauce in a small bowl. Set the bowl aside. Season the beef strips with a generous grinding of black pepper.

When the browning dish is heated, brush ½ tablespoon of the oil evenly over the dish to coat it. Sear half of the beef strips on the dish, stirring and turning the meat with a wooden spoon. Once the beef has been seared—after

1 or 2 minutes—transfer it to a browning dish. Wipe off the browning dish with a paper towel and reheat it for 3 minutes. Brush the remaining oil on to the dish and sear the remaining beef in the same way. Add the beef to the baking dish.

Add the spring onions, carrot and red pepper to the beef. Pour the sauce over all and microwave the mixture on high for 3 minutes. Serve the beef and vegetables from the baking dish or transfer them to a platter; serve at once.

Escalopes in Tarragon and Mushroom Sauce

Serves 4

Working time: about 15 minutes

Total time: about 1 hour and 15 minutes

Calories 240
Protein 22g
Cholesterol 100mg
Total fat 11g
Saturated fat 3g
Sodium 215mg

4	thin veal escalopes (about 125 g/4 oz each)	4
2 tbsp	virgin olive oil	2 tbsp
2 tbsp	finely shredded fresh tarragon leaves	2 tbsp
	freshly ground black pepper	

Mushroom sauce		
175 g	mushrooms, trimmed and sliced	6 oz
4 tbsp	Marsala	4 tbsp
15 g	plain flour	$\frac{1}{2}$ oz
2 tbsp	soured cream mixed with skimmed milk to make 15 cl ($\frac{1}{4}$ pint)	2 tbsp
$\frac{1}{4}$ tsp	salt	$\frac{1}{4}$ tsp

Blend the oil with 1 tablespoon of the tarragon and some pepper in a shallow dish. Add the escalopes and turn them in the oil until they are evenly coated. Cover the dish and leave to marinate at room temperature for 1 hour.

Heat a browning dish on high for the maximum time allowed in the instruction manual. Brown the escalopes on each side in the hot dish, then cover and microwave on high for 1$\frac{1}{2}$ minutes. Transfer the escalopes to a plate, cover and set aside.

To make the sauce, stir the Marsala into the browning dish, add the mushrooms and microwave on high for 2 minutes. Blend the flour with the soured cream mixture, remaining tarragon, salt and a little black pepper until smooth. Stir into the mushrooms and microwave on high for 1 minute. Return the escalopes to the dish, coat well with the sauce and microwave for 2$\frac{1}{2}$ to 3 minutes, repositioning the escalopes half way through cooking. Serve immediately.

Veal with Green Peppercorns and Tomato Sauce

Serves 6

Working time:
about 20
minutes

Total time:
about 1 hour
and 20 minutes
(includes
marinating)

Calories
150

Protein
22g

Cholesterol
90mg

Total fat
6g

Saturated fat
2g

Sodium
180mg

6	medallions of veal (about 125 g/ 4 oz each), trimmed and neatly tied	**6**	**2 tsp**	mixed dried herbs	**2 tsp**
1 tbsp	virgin olive oil	**1 tbsp**	**1**	garlic clove, crushed	**1**
1 tsp	dried green peppercorns, crushed	**1 tsp**	**¼ tsp**	salt	**¼ tsp**
2 tbsp	brandy	**2 tbsp**		freshly ground black pepper	
350 g	ripe tomatoes, skinned, seeded and chopped	**12 oz**		watercress for garnish	

Mix the oil with the peppercorns in a shallow dish, add the medallions and turn them in the oil until they are coated. Cover and allow to marinate at room temperature for 1 hour.

Heat a browning dish on high for the maximum time allowed in the instruction manual. Brown the medallions on both sides in the hot dish, then cover and microwave on high for 3 minutes, turning them over after 1½ minutes. Transfer the meat to a serving plate, cover with foil and set aside.

Stir the brandy into the browning dish and microwave on high for 1 minute, or until reduced by half.

Add the tomatoes, garlic, herbs, salt and pepper. Cover and microwave on high for 4 minutes, stirring frequently. Pour into a hot serving jug or bowl. Meanwhile, microwave the medallions on high for 1 minute more to heat through. Garnish with watercress and serve immediately with the tomato sauce.

Medallions of Veal and Yogurt-Lemon Vegetables

Serves 6

Working time:
about 30
minutes

Total time:
about 1 hour
(includes
marinating)

Calories
190

Protein
24g

Cholesterol
90mg

Total fat
8g

Saturated fat
2g

Sodium
190mg

6	medallions of veal (about 125 g/4 oz each), trimmed and neatly tied	6
2 tbsp	virgin olive oil	2 tbsp
1	garlic clove, crushed	1
	freshly ground black pepper	
2	small onions, quartered	2
4	asparagus spears, trimmed and thinly sliced diagonally	4

125 g	button mushrooms, stems trimmed	4 oz
125 g	frozen peas	4 oz
15 g	flour	½ oz
1	lemon, finely grated rind only	1
¼ tsp	salt	¼ tsp
3 tbsp	plain low-fat yogurt	3 tbsp
	lemon wedges and parsley for garnish (optional)	

In a shallow dish, mix 1 tablespoon of the oil with the garlic and some pepper. Add the medallions and coat with the oil. Cover and marinate at room temperature for 30 minutes.

About 15 minutes before cooking the medallions, put the remaining oil into a shallow dish and microwave on high for 30 seconds. Add the onions and asparagus, cover and microwave on high for 4 minutes, stirring after 2 minutes. Add the mushrooms and peas, cover and microwave on high for 6 minutes, stirring after 3 minutes. Meanwhile, blend the flour with the lemon rind, salt, some pepper and the yogurt. Stir into the vegetables and microwave

on high for 3 minutes, stirring after each minute. Remove from the microwave and keep warm.

Heat a browning dish on high for the maximum time allowed. Brown both sides of the medallions in the hot dish. Cover and microwave on high for 1 ½ minutes, then turn the medallions over and microwave for a further 1 minute. Remove the meat to a hot serving dish, cover with foil and allow to stand for 1 minute.

Meanwhile, microwave the cooked vegetables on high for 1 minute to heat through. Serve the medallions, garnished with the lemon wedges and parsley.

Meatballs with Sweet Pepper Sauce

Serves 4

Working (and total) time: about 1 hour

Calories 280
Protein 26g
Cholesterol 90mg
Total fat 12g
Saturated fat 4g
Sodium 385mg

500 g	veal rump, trimmed of fat and very finely minced	**1 lb**		**Red and green pepper sauce**	
90 g	brown breadcrumbs	**3 oz**	**1**	onion, thinly sliced	**1**
1	small onion, finely chopped	**1**	**1**	small sweet red pepper, thinly sliced	**1**
2 tbsp	chopped parsley	**2 tbsp**	**1**	small sweet green pepper, sliced	**1**
1 tsp	mixed dried herbs	**1 tsp**	**3**	sticks celery, thinly sliced	**3**
2 tbsp	virgin olive oil	**2 tbsp**	**2 tsp**	paprika	**2 tsp**
1	egg white	**1**	**2 tsp**	tomato paste	**2 tsp**
	freshly ground black pepper		**30 cl**	unsalted veal or chicken stock	**½ pint**
			¼ tsp	salt	**¼ tsp**

Place the veal in a bowl with the breadcrumbs, chopped onion, parsley, herbs, 1 tablespoon of the oil and the egg white. Season with black pepper, then mix them all thoroughly together until smooth. Divide the mixture into 20 equal-sized pieces and roll each piece into a neat ball.

Heat a browning dish on high for the maximum time allowed in the instruction manual. Add the remaining oil to the dish. Put the meatballs into the oil and microwave on high, uncovered, for 5 to 6 minutes, turning and repositioning them every 2 minutes. Transfer them to a plate and set aside.

To make the sauce, add the sliced onion, sweet red and green peppers and celery to the oil remaining in the browning dish and stir. Microwave on high, uncovered, for 4 to 5 minutes, until the vegetables are softened. Stir in the paprika and microwave for 30 seconds. Stir in the tomato paste, stock and salt. Cover the dish and microwave on high for 8 minutes, stirring every 2 minutes.

Return the meatballs to the dish, coat them well with the sauce, then microwave on high for 2 minutes. Serve immediately.

Pork and Spinach Pie

Serves 6 as a main course

Working time: about 30 minutes

Total time: about 1 hour

Calories 300

Protein 22g

Cholesterol 85mg

Total fat 11g

Saturated fat 4g

Sodium 570mg

300 g	frozen chopped spinach	**10 oz**
250 g	pork fillet, trimmed and chopped	**8 oz**
1 tsp	fennel seeds	**1 tsp**
2	garlic cloves, finely chopped	**2**
1 tsp	ground coriander	**1 tsp**
½ tsp	salt	**½ tsp**
1 tbsp	virgin olive oil	**1 tbsp**

½ tsp	dried hot red pepper flakes	**½ tsp**
60 cl	butter milk	**1 pint**
1	egg, plus 1 egg white	**1**
1	loaf French bread (about 250 g/ 8 oz), cut into 1 cm (½ inch) thick slices	**1**
60 g	Parmesan cheese, freshly grated	**2 oz**

Set the frozen spinach on a plate and microwave on high for 2½ minutes. Set aside.

Mix together the pork, fennel seeds, garlic, coriander, salt, ½ tablespoon of the oil and ¼ teaspoon of the red pepper flakes. In another bowl, mix the buttermilk, egg and egg white, the remaining oil and red pepper flakes.

Spread the bread in a single layer in a shallow baking tray. Pour on all but 4 tablespoons of the buttermilk mixture, then turn the bread. Let the bread stand, turning the slices frequently until it has absorbed nearly all the liquid—about 15 minutes.

Microwave the pork mixture on high for 1½ minutes, stirring once at midpoint. Remove the

spinach from the package and squeeze it to remove as much liquid as possible. Stir into the pork mixture, with the reserved buttermilk mixture and half of the cheese.

Spoon a quarter of the pork mixture into a 28 cm (11 inch) glass pie plate. Layer half of the bread on top. Cover the bread with half of the remaining pork mixture and top this layer with the remaining bread. Spread the remaining pork. Cover.

Microwave on medium for 4 minutes. Rotate the dish half way and cook it for another 4 minutes. Uncover the dish and scatter on the remaining cheese. Cook 8 minutes more. Let the dish stand for 5 minutes before serving it.

Spaghetti Squash with Basil and Pine-Nuts

Serves 6

Working time: about 10 minutes

Total time: about 40 minutes

Calories
105
Protein
3g
Cholesterol
1mg
Total fat
3g
Saturated fat
0g
Sodium
80mg

1	spaghetti squash (about 2 kg/4 lb)	**1**
4 tbsp	unsalted chicken stock or water	**4 tbsp**
1	ripe tomato, skinned, seeded and cut into small dice	**1**
4 tbsp	chopped fresh basil	**4 tbsp**
2 tbsp	pine-nuts, toasted in a dry frying pan over medium heat	**2 tbsp**
2 tbsp	freshly grated Parmesan cheese	**2 tbsp**
1 tsp	fresh lemon juice	**1 tsp**
1 tbsp	caster sugar	**1 tbsp**
1	whole basil leaf for garnish	**1**

Pierce the squash several times with the point of a sharp knife. Put the squash into a shallow casserole and microwave it on high for 20 minutes, turning it over half way through the cooking. Remove the squash from the oven and let it stand for 10 minutes.

Cut the squash in half lengthwise; remove and discard the seeds. Using a fork, remove the flesh of the squash and put it into a bowl.

Add the stock or water, tomato, chopped basil, pine-nuts, Parmesan cheese, lemon juice and sugar and toss them all together. Microwave the mixture on high for 4 minutes. Remove the squash from the oven and let it cool slightly. Put the squash into a serving dish and garnish the dish with the basil leaf, if you are using it. Serve the squash at once.

Broccoli Steamed with Orange and Caraway

Serves 4

Working time:
about 15
minutes

Total time:
about 25
minutes

Calories
95
Protein
6g
Cholesterol
10mg
Total fat
4g
Saturated fat
2g
Sodium
160mg

500 g	broccoli, stalks trimmed to within 5 cm (2 inches) of the florets	**1 lb**	
12.5 cl	unsalted chicken or vegetable stock	**4 fl oz**	
1	orange, juice only of one half, other half peeled and divided into segments	**1**	
15 g	unsalted butter	**$\frac{1}{2}$ oz**	
1 tbsp	flour	**1 tbsp**	
2 tsp	caraway seeds	**2 tsp**	
$\frac{1}{4}$ tsp	salt	**$\frac{1}{4}$ tsp**	
	freshly ground black pepper		

Peel any broccoli stalk that is more than 1 cm ($\frac{1}{2}$ inch) thick and split its base 1 cm ($\frac{1}{2}$ inch) deep.

In a small bowl, combine the stock and orange juice. Put the butter in a shallow baking dish and microwave it on high until it is melted—about 30 seconds. Whisk the flour into the butter to form a paste. Pour the stock and orange juice into the flour paste and stir until the mixture is smooth. Microwave the sauce on high for 1 $\frac{1}{2}$ minutes, stir it, then microwave it on high for another 1 $\frac{1}{2}$ minutes.

Stir in the orange segments, caraway seeds, salt and pepper. Arrange the broccoli on top of the sauce with the florets towards the centre. Cover the dish with plastic film, leaving one corner open, and microwave it on high for 7 minutes more. Then let the dish stand covered until the broccoli is tender—3 to 4 minutes.

Transfer the broccoli to a serving dish. Stir the sauce well, then pour it evenly over the broccoli and serve.

Creamed Spinach with Shiitake Mushrooms

Serves 4

Working time: about 30 minutes

Total time: about 40 minutes

Calories 75

Protein 3g

Cholesterol 15mg

Total fat 5g

Saturated fat 3g

Sodium 185mg

650 g	spinach, washed, stems removed	**1½ lb**
1 tbsp	flour	**1 tbsp**
12.5 cl	unsalted chicken or vegetable stock	**4 fl oz**
60 g	shiitake mushrooms, stems removed, caps wiped and sliced	**2 oz**

6 cl	milk	**2 fl oz**
⅛ tsp	grated nutmeg	**⅛ tsp**
¼ tsp	salt	**¼ tsp**
	freshly ground black pepper	
25 g	unsalted butter	**¾ oz**

Put the spinach in a large baking dish and cover it tightly with plastic film. Pierce the film to allow steam to escape. Microwave the spinach on high until it is wilted and tender—about 4 minutes. Transfer it to a colander and pour off any liquid in the dish.

Melt the butter in the baking dish by microwaving it on high for 30 seconds. Whisk the flour into the butter until a smooth paste results, then whisk in the stock. Add the mushrooms to this sauce and cover the dish again with plastic film, pierced as before. Microwave on high until the sauce bubbles—about 2 minutes.

Squeeze the excess moisture from the spinach. Coarsely chop the spinach and add it to the sauce along with the milk, nutmeg, salt and pepper. Mix well to coat the spinach thoroughly with the sauce. Microwave on high for 2 minutes more. Let the dish stand for 2 to 3 minutes before serving.

Savoury Pumpkin Flans

Serves 6

Working time: about 20 minutes

Total time: about 40 minutes

Calories 120
Protein 4g
Cholesterol 10mg
Total fat 6g
Saturated fat 3g
Sodium 35mg

1	small pumpkin (about 1 kg/2½ lb), halved horizontally, seeds removed	1	1 tbsp	brown sugar	1 tbsp
30 g	unsalted butter	1 oz	¼ tsp	cinnamon	¼ tsp
30 g	flour	1 oz	¼ tsp	grated nutmeg	¼ tsp
3 tbsp	evaporated milk	3 tbsp	¼ tsp	vanilla extract	¼ tsp
3	egg whites	3	1	lemon, grated rind only	1
			2 tbsp	chopped walnuts	2 tbsp

Cut each pumpkin half into four wedges. Place these in a shallow baking dish, cover them with plastic film, pierce the film and microwave them on high for 6 minutes. Rearrange the wedges so that their less-cooked portions face the outside of the dish. Cover the pumpkin once again and microwave on high until the flesh is tender—4 to 6 minutes. Let the wedges stand until they are cool enough to handle.

Scoop out the pumpkin flesh and purée it in a food processor. There should be about ½ litre (16 fl oz) of purée.

In a bowl, microwave the butter on high for 30 seconds. Stir in the flour to make a smooth paste. Whisk in the evaporated milk and egg whites. Stir into the purée with the brown

sugar, cinnamon, nutmeg, vanilla and lemon rind.

Butter the bottoms of six 17.5 cl (6 fl oz) ramekins. Spoon the pumpkin mixture into the ramekins and arrange them in a circle in the microwave. Cook the pumpkin flans on medium high (70 per cent power) until they start to pull away from the sides of the ramekins—about 10 minutes.

Let the flans stand for 5 minutes before unmoulding them. Loosen a flan by running a knife around the inside of the ramekin. Invert the ramekin on to a plate and rap the bottom of the mould; lift away the mould. Repeat the process to unmould the other flans. Sprinkle the flans with the walnuts before serving.

Leafy Layer

Serves 6

Working time: about 35 minutes

Total time: about 1 hour

Calories 90
Protein 10g
Cholesterol 150mg
Total fat 2g
Saturated fat 1g
Sodium 210mg

6 or 7	large leaves from a green cabbage	6 or 7
250 g	spinach, stems removed	8 oz
250 g	Swiss chard, white stems removed	8 oz
250 g	leeks, trimmed and thinly sliced	8 oz
125 g	sorrel, finely shredded	4 oz
2	eggs	2
1	egg white	1
30 cl	skimmed milk	½ pint
¼ tsp	salt	¼ tsp
	freshly ground black pepper	
1 tbsp	chopped tarragon	1 tbsp
2 tbsp	finely chopped parsley	2 tbsp
2	spring onions, finely chopped	2

Trim away the protruding rib at the back of each cabbage leaf until it is level with the rest of the leaf. Wash cabbage leaves, spinach, chard, leeks and sorrel very thoroughly, keeping each vegetable separate.

Place the cabbage leaves in a large bowl. Cover with plastic film, leaving one corner open. Microwave on high just long enough to soften the leaves—3 to 4 minutes. Remove the leaves and drain them well on kitchen paper. Repeat with the spinach, chard and leeks.

Put the eggs, egg white, milk, salt and pepper into a mixing bowl. Whisk them lightly together, then stir in the herbs and spring onions.

Very lightly butter a deep, round dish, about 20 (8 inches) in diameter and 5 cm (2 inches) deep. Neatly line the dish with some of the cabbage leaves, overlapping them to ensure a snug fit and allowing excess leaf to overhang at the top of the dish.

Fill the lined dish with alternate layers of spinach, chard, leeks, sorrel and herb custard mixture. Place remaining cabbage leaves on top of the filling, bring the overhanging leaves in over the top to enclose the filling.

Cover the dish with plastic film, leaving one corner open. Microwave on high until the custard is just set—18 to 20 minutes. Allow to stand for 5 minutes, then carefully unmould on to a hot serving plate.

Chocolate Bombes

Makes 12
bombes

Working time:
about 45
minutes

Total time:
about 3 hours
(includes
chilling)

Per bombe:
Calories
150
Protein
5g
Cholesterol
15mg
Total fat
9g
Saturated fat
5g
Sodium
140mg

250 g	low-fat cottage cheese	**8 oz**
30 g	caster sugar	**1 oz**
4 tbsp	whipping cream	**4 tbsp**
$\frac{1}{2}$	lemon, grated rind only	$\frac{1}{2}$
30 g	glacé cherries, finely chopped	**1 oz**
30 g	glacé ginger, finely chopped	**1 oz**
1 tbsp	Tia Maria	**1 tbsp**

30 g	shelled walnuts, finely chopped	**1 oz**
2.5 cm	cube crystallized ginger,	**1 inch**
	chopped, to decorate	
	Chocolate coating	
90 g	plain chocolate	**3 oz**
45 g	unsalted butter	**1$\frac{1}{2}$oz**

Sieve the cottage cheese into a bowl, add the caster sugar and whipping cream, and whisk with an electric mixer until very light. Divide between two bowls. Add the lemon rind, glacé cherries and chopped ginger to one bowl. Stir the Tia Maria and chopped walnuts into the other bowl. Set aside.

Use plastic egg boxes as moulds for the bombes. Line 12 moulds with pieces of plastic film. Distribute the glacé cherry and ginger mixture among the moulds, smooth the surfaces, then spoon on the nut and Tia Maria mixture and smooth again. Chill for 2 hours.

To make the coating, put the chocolate and butter into a small bowl and microwave them on medium until the chocolate has melted—3 to 4 minutes. Stir until smooth, then leave to cool until almost beginning to set.

Unmould the bombes on to a board and remove the plastic film. Slide a metal spatula under each bombe, hold it over the bowl of melted chocolate and carefully spoon the mixture over the bombe, spreading it with a knife to ensure an even coating. Set the bombe on a wire rack and score the surface of the chocolate coating with the tines of a fork. Decorate each one with a piece of crystallized ginger.

Serve the bombes when the chocolate coating has completely set—10 to 15 minutes.

Chocolate and Ginger Cheesecakes

Makes 6 cheesecakes

Working time: about 30 minutes

Total time: about 3 hours (includes chilling)

Per cheesecake:
Calories
210
Protein
10g
Cholesterol
10mg
Total fat
9g
Saturated fat
5g
Sodium
230mg

45 g	digestive biscuits	**1½oz**
75 g	plain chocolate	**2½oz**
2 tsp	powdered gelatine	**2 tsp**
2 tbsp	clear honey	**2 tbsp**

30 g	crystallized ginger	**1 oz**
300 g	quark	**10 oz**
6 cl	single cream	**2 fl oz**
1 tsp	icing sugar, to decorate	**1 tsp**

Cut six circles of greaseproof paper to line the bases of six 12.5 cl (4 fl oz) ramekins. Break the biscuits into pieces, and process them briefly in a food processor. Break 45 g (1½oz) of the chocolate into a basin and microwave it on medium for 2½to 3 minutes, until melted. Stir until smooth, then combine with the biscuit crumbs.Press into the bases of the ramekins. Chill until firm.

Sprinkle the gelatine over 2 tablespoons of water in a bowl and leave it for 2 minutes. Microwave on high for 30 seconds, to melt the gelatine. Stir in the honey and cool slightly.

Meanwhile, very finely chop the ginger in a food processor and combine it with the quark and cream. Mix together until smooth, then blend in the gelatine mixture thoroughly. Divide among the ramekins, cover with plastic film and chill for at least 2 hours, or preferably overnight, until set.

For the topping, break the remaining chocolate into a basin and microwave it on medium for 2 to 2½minutes. Stir the chocolate until smooth, then, using a metal spatula, spread it out very thinly on a marble slab or an inverted baking sheet. Leave to cool for 3 to 4 minutes, until almost set. Push a pastry scraper under the chocolate to produce scrolls.

Just before serving, slip a knife round the sides of the ramekins. Carefully unmould each cheesecake into the palm of your hand—to remove the lining paper—then place it on a board. Cover the cheesecakes with chocolate scrolls. Using a metal spatula to cover half the top of each cheesecake, sift icing sugar over the other half.

Pear and Hazelnut Galettes

Makes 8 galettes

Working time: about 30 minutes

Total time: about 1 hour

Per galette:
Calories 175
Protein 1g
Cholesterol 30mg
Total fat 5g
Saturated fat 2g
Sodium 15mg

2	Conference pears	2
15 cl	port	**¼ pint**
90 g	caster sugar	**3 oz**
15 g	glacé ginger, finely chopped	**½ oz**
6 tbsp	pastry cream	**6 tbsp**

Hazelnut shortbread

30 g	unsalted butter	**1 oz**
15 g	castersugar	**½ oz**
45 g	plain flour	**1½ oz**
15 g	shelled hazelnuts, toasted and skinned, finely ground	**½ oz**

Peel and core the pears then cut them into long, thin slices.

Combine the port and sugar in a 20 cm (8 inch) shallow round dish. Microwave on high for 2 minutes, then stir until the sugar has dissolved. Coat the pear slices in the syrup. Cover with plastic film, leaving a corner open to allow steam to escape. Cook the pears on high, giving the dish a quarter turn after 3 minutes, until tender—6 to 8 minutes. Loosen the plastic film and drain the syrup into a heatproof bowl. Leave the pears to cool.

Heat the syrup on high until it has become quite thick and smells slightly of caramel—about 7 minutes—then set it aside to cool.

Meanwhile, cream together the butter and sugar, then mix in the flour and hazelnuts to make a stiff dough. Turn on to a lightly floured work surface and roll to a thickness of about 3 mm (⅛ inch). Using a 7.5 cm (3 inch) plain cutter, cut out eight circles. Place a sheet of non-stick parchment paper in the microwave. Put four shortbread circles on the paper and cook on high for 2 minutes. Cool slightly, before placing them on a wire rack and cooking the second batch.

Stir the ginger into the pastry cream. Spoon a little on to each of the shortbread circles, spreading it quite close to the edge. Arrange a few pear slices on each base. Dribble the thickened syrup over the pears. Serve immediately.

Chocolate Boxes

Makes 18 boxes

Working time: about 1 hour

Total time: about 1 hour and 30 minutes

Per box:
Calories 70
Protein 2g
Cholesterol 40mg
Total fat 3g
Saturated fat 1g
Sodium 20mg

1	egg	**1**	**1 tbsp**	kirsch	**1 tbsp**
45 g	caster sugar	**1½ oz**	**30 cl**	pastry cream	**½ pint**
45 g	plain flour	**1½ oz**	**5**	strawberries, hulled and quartered lengthwise	**5**
60 g	plain chocolate, broken into pieces	**2 oz**			

Line the base of an 18 by 10 by 4 cm (7 by 4 by 1½ inch) dish with greaseproof paper. Put the egg and sugar into a mixing bowl and whisk until the mixture is very thick and pale, and falls from the whisk in a ribbon trail. Sift the flour lightly over the whisked mixture, then fold it in gently with a metal spoon. Pour the batter into the prepared dish, tipping the dish to distribute it evenly. Microwave on high for about 50 seconds (the top of the sponge should still be slightly moist). Set the sponge aside.

Meanwhile, start making the chocolate squares. Grease a 30 by 15 cm (12 by 6 inch) tin and line it with waxed paper. Place the chocolate in a small bowl and microwave on medium for 2½ to 3 minutes, until the chocolate has melted, then pour it into the prepared tin,

spread it evenly with a metal spatula and leave to set in a cool place—about 30 minutes.

Invert the cooled sponge on to a board and remove the paper. Using a sharp knife, trim all four sides to obtain neat straight edges. Then cut the sponge rectangle into 18 squares slightly smaller than 2.5 cm (1 inch), and discard the excess. Cut the chocolate into 72 squares measuring 2.5 cm (1 inch) each.

Stir the kirsch into the pastry cream. Using a round bladed knife, spread a little of the pastry cream on the sides of the sponges and press a chocolate square to each side. Transfer the remaining pastry cream to a piping bag fitted with a medium star nozzle. Pipe two lines of cream across each box and place a strawberry quarter on top.

Banana Diamonds

Makes 12 diamonds

Working time: about 40 minutes

Total time: about 1 hour and 15 minutes

Per diamond:
Calories 190
Protein 4g
Cholesterol 20mg
Total fat 6g
Saturated fat 1g
Sodium 180mg

175 g	wholemeal flour	**6 oz**
½ tsp	bicarbonate of soda	**½ tsp**
125 g	light brown sugar	**4 oz**
4 tbsp	skimmed milk	**4 tbsp**
2	ripe bananas, mashed	**2**
4 tbsp	safflower or sunflower oil	**4 tbsp**
1	egg	**1**
½ tsp	baking powder	**½ tsp**
½ tsp	pure vanilla extract	**½ tsp**
2 tbsp	icing sugar, to decorate	**2 tbsp**
	Cheese filling	
200 g	low-fat soft cheese	**7 oz**
3 tbsp	icing sugar	**3 tbsp**
3½ tbsp	fresh orange juice	**3½ tbsp**
1 tsp	mixed spice	**1 tsp**

Line the base of a 28 by 18 cm (11 by 7 inch) rectangular dish with parchment paper.

Put the flour and bicarbonate of soda into a bowl, mix in the brown sugar, then the milk, bananas, oil, egg, baking powder and vanilla extract. Beat until smooth, then turn it into the lined dish and microwave on medium for 6 minutes, giving a half turn every 2 minutes. Increase to high and microwave until springy but still moist—4 to 5 minutes. Remove the cake from the oven and leave to cool.

To make the filling, combine the cheese, sugar, orange juice and mixed spice in a bowl.

Place the cake on a work surface and trim to make a neat rectangle. Cut horizontally through the cake to give two equal layers. Spread the filling evenly over the bottom layer. Replace the top layer and cut the cake lengthwise into three equal strips. Cut each strip diagonally into four diamond shapes.

Using stiff paper, cut out a diamond-shaped template the size of one of the banana diamonds. Draw a large X across the middle, making four small diamonds. Cut out two facing diamonds. Place the template on one of the banana diamonds and sprinkle it with the icing sugar. Remove the template and repeat with the rest of the cakes.

Amaretto Meringues

Makes 32
meringues

Working
(and total)
time: about
20 minutes

Per meringue:
Calories
65
Protein
1g
Cholesterol
15mg
Total fat
2g
Saturated fat
trace
Sodium
10mg

1	egg white	**1**
300 g	icing sugar	**10 oz**
⅛ tsp	pure almond extract	**⅛ tsp**

30 g	flaked almonds	**1 oz**
1 tbsp	amaretto liqueur	**1 tbsp**
30 cl	pastry cream	**½ pint**

Put the egg white into a bowl, sift in the icing sugar and add the almond extract. Stir the mixture until it is very stiff and firm; if it is sticky, add a little more icing sugar—about 1 teaspoon.

Using your fingers, shape the mixture into 64 small balls of about ½ teaspoon of mixture each. Place eight balls, spaced well apart, in a circle on non-stick parchment paper. Using your thumb, lightly flatten each ball, and press a few flaked almonds into the top of each. Microwave the balls on high for 1 minute, giving the paper a quarter turn every 20 seconds; the meringues will increase in size until they measure about 6 cm (2½ inches), and

should hold their shape when cooked—if they collapse when the oven door is opened, cook them for a further 20 seconds.

Remove the meringues from the oven, allow to cool for 1 minute, then carefully lift them off the paper and place them on a wire rack to finish cooling. Continue preparing and cooking the balls in batches of eight.

Stir the amaretto into the pastry cream. Using a round-bladed knife, spread about 1 tablespoon of flavoured pastry cream on to the flat surface of a meringue, then gently press the flat surface of a second meringue into the cream. Arrange the filled meringues on a serving plate and serve them immediately.

Useful weights and measures

Weight Equivalents

Avoirdupois		Metric
1 ounce	=	28.35 grams
1 pound	=	254.6 grams
2.3 pounds	=	1 kilogram

Liquid Measurements

$^1/_4$ pint	=	$1^1/_2$ decilitres
$^1/_2$ pint	=	$^1/_4$ litre
scant 1 pint	=	$^1/_2$ litre
$1^3/_4$ pints	=	1 litre
1 gallon	=	4.5 litres

Liquid Measures

1 pint	= 20 fl oz	= 32 tablespoons
$^1/_2$ pint	= 10 fl oz	= 16 tablespoons
$^1/_4$ pint	= 5 fl oz	= 8 tablespoons
$^1/_8$ pint	= $2^1/_2$ fl oz	= 4 tablespoons
$^1/_{16}$ pint	= $1^1/_4$ fl oz	= 2 tablespoons

Solid Measures

1 oz almonds, ground = $3^3/_4$ level tablespoons
1 oz breadcrumbs fresh = 7 level tablespoons
1 oz butter, lard = 2 level tablespoons
1 oz cheese, grated = $3^1/_2$ level tablespoons
1 oz cocoa = $2^3/_4$ level tablespoons
1 oz desiccated coconut = $4^1/_2$ tablespoons
1 oz cornflour = $2^1/_2$ tablespoons
1 oz custard powder = $2^1/_2$ tablespoons
1 oz curry powder and spices = 5 tablespoons
1 oz flour = 2 level tablespoons
1 oz rice, uncooked = $1^1/_2$ tablespoons
1 oz sugar, caster and granulated = 2 tablespoons
1 oz icing sugar = $2^1/_2$ tablespoons
1 oz yeast, granulated = 1 level tablespoon

American Measures

16 fl oz	=1 American pint
8 fl oz	=1 American standard cup
0.50 fl oz	=1 American tablespoon

(*slightly smaller than British Standards Institute tablespoon*)

0.16 fl oz	=1 American teaspoon

Australian Cup Measures
(*Using the 8-liquid-ounce cup measure*)

1 cup flour	4 oz
1 cup sugar (crystal or caster)	8 oz
1 cup icing sugar (free from lumps)	5 oz
1 cup shortening (butter, margarine)	8 oz
1 cup brown sugar (lightly packed)	4 oz
1 cup soft breadcrumbs	2 oz
1 cup dry breadcrumbs	3 oz
1 cup rice (uncooked)	6 oz
1 cup rice (cooked)	5 oz
1 cup mixed fruit	4 oz
1 cup grated cheese	4 oz
1 cup nuts (chopped)	4 oz
1 cup coconut	$2^1/_2$ oz

Australian Spoon Measures

	level tablespoon
1 oz flour	2
1 oz sugar	$1^1/_2$
1 oz icing sugar	2
1 oz shortening	1
1 oz honey	1
1 oz gelatine	2
1 oz cocoa	3
1 oz cornflour	$2^1/_2$
1 oz custard powder	$2^1/_2$

Australian Liquid Measures
(*Using 8-liquid-ounce cup*)

1 cup liquid	8 oz
$2^1/_2$ cups liquid	20 oz (1 pint)
2 tablespoons liquid	1 oz
1 gill liquid	5 oz ($^1/_4$ pint)